Foreword

I hope you enjoy this book as much as I enjoyed writing it. I didn't know if this book would someday be published or not. That was not my reason for writing it. Many people–friends, relatives and acquaintances–had suggested that I should write a book about my years of being such a die-hard Buckeye fan. At family gatherings, church functions and other occasions people have been impressed with my memories of growing up in Columbus and rooting for my beloved Buckeyes. Most of what you will read in this book was a result of my excellent memory with a few facts coming from other sources. Those sources were as follows: Ohio State Media Guides, Buckeye Sports Bulletins, "Greatest Moments in Ohio State Football," "Ohio State 100 Years of Football," and various web sites i.e. Penn State, Michigan, Oklahoma, West Virginia and others.

Acknowledgements

I would like to acknowledge the following for their assistance in making this book a reality.

Cheryl and Keith Johnson, Todd Skipton, Ann Mirels, my daughter Lisa Spencer, and my wife Marty Hansgen.

S0-AAZ-751

A Buckeye Remembers

by

Larry C. Hansgen

Go Bucks!

Larry C. Hansgen

2012

Go Bucks,
Dave!
Yer
Lester

Published by *Skye's The Limit Publishing & Public Relations*

Books published by Skye's The Limit Publishing & Public Relations may be available at special discounts for bulk purchases in the United States by corporations, institutions, and other organizations. For more information, please contact the Marketing Department at Skye's The Limit Publishing & Public Relations, P.O. Box 133, Galena, Ohio 43021, (fax) 740-548-4929; or via e-mail at talk2us@stl.skyemarie.com

Cover, design, and typography by Cheryl A. Johnson

Skye's the Limit Publishing & Public Relations
PO Box 133, Galena, Ohio 43021
(fax) 740-548-4929
stlpublishing.skyemarie.com

Published in the United States of America.

Paperback:
    ISBN-13: 978-1-939044-00-6
    ISBN-10: 1939044006

eBook:
    ISBN-13: 978-1-939044-01-3

Author Blog: abuckeyeremembers.blogspot.com

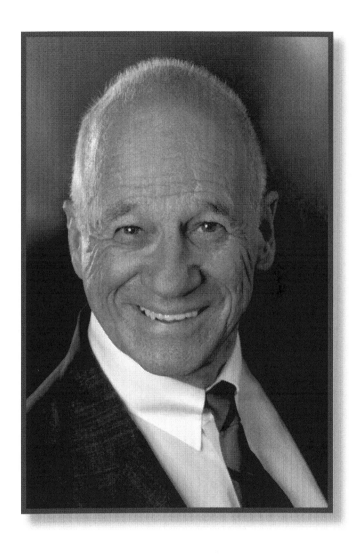

iii

Table of Contents

The Early Years

I was born on Thursday, April 18, 1935. That was the first notable event of that year. The hospital was, of course, The Ohio State University Hospital, and just northwest of the hospital near the east bank of the Olentangy River was a huge gray edifice that came into being just 13 years before my birth. It would prove to be an important part of the life of the first and only child born to Lawrence and Ruth Hansgen. They named him Larry Clayton, not junior, as his name was not Lawrence. In those days Larry became a proper name in its own right, not a nickname for Lawrence. This would cause many disputes during my life. I even had a teacher, Mrs. Murer, who stated, "Your name is Lawrence and I will not use nicknames in my class." She told a fellow student, Jim Welch, that his name was James not Jim. We both brought our birth certificates to prove to her that we were really Larry and Jim, not Lawrence and James.

That huge edifice was the Ohio Stadium and the second notable event of 1935 was one of the greatest games of all time that took place that fall within the gray horseshoe. The Buckeyes lost a heartbreaker to Notre Dame by a score of 18 to 13. I would have loved to have been present at that game, but I was only six months old. The Irish prevailed again the next year in South Bend 7 to 2. They didn't meet again until 1995 and I was there as the Bucks avenged their loss of 60 years earlier. The final score was 46 to 25, as the Irish couldn't cope with the speed of the Buckeyes. Unheralded Terry Glenn burned the Irish secondary and Eddie George took a giant step towards the Heisman Trophy with an outstanding game on national TV.

I grew up in the area south of OSU which is known today as the short north. I lived on Second Avenue in a house that has since been torn down due to gentrification. I attended Michigan Avenue Elementary School which was located two blocks from my house at the corner of Michigan Avenue and Fourth Avenue. It later became Fourth Avenue Elementary School and today is a residence for Senior Citizens. Until I became a big Buckeye fan it didn't bother me to attend a school named Michigan. I believe I was in the fourth grade when I attended my first OSU game as a Cub Scout. For the next two years I wished that my school had any name but the one that was our arch rival's.

In that game OSU trounced Pittsburgh and running back Ollie Cline became my favorite player. The next year he set the OSU record when he rushed for 229 yards at Pittsburgh. That record stood for 27 years until a freshman from Columbus Eastmoor rushed for 239 yards against North Carolina in the Horseshoe. That freshman was Archie Griffin who would break that record the next year when he rushed for 246 yards against the Iowa Hawkeyes in Columbus. Eleven years later that record was broken by Keith Byars when he gained 274 yards in a come from behind win over Illinois in Ohio Stadium. Eleven years later guess who broke that record? It was tailback Eddie George when he ran for 314 yards and once again it was against the Fighting Illini in the giant horseshoe.

I used to play football on a neighborhood team made up of guys that lived in my area and we would play guys that lived south of our area. We played at North Field, a large field that was located on Fifth Avenue near the Olentangy River. It covered an area between Fifth Avenue and King Avenue. It contained two ball diamonds, two football fields and a playground area. It is now part of the Battelle complex.

Although I loved the game I wasn't very talented and was always small for my age. I took my share of bumps and bruises playing against bigger and more talented kids. However, it never deterred my love and desire for the game. My dream was to play when I got to high school. When I started tenth grade at Central High School I was four foot nine inches tall and weighed 90 lbs. Three years later when I graduated I was five foot eight and weighed 120 lbs. I tried everything to get bigger and stronger. I lifted weights and drank milk shakes but I remained trapped in a kid's body. In my first year of high school, students used to say to me, "Hey kid, you go to school here?" Some of those guys had muscles and were shaving and I still looked like an elementary student.

My buddies and I used to go up to the Horseshoe and sneak in by climbing over the gates at the south end of the stadium. I never climbed over the gates because I was little enough to squeeze through the bars on the gate. One day I got my head caught between the bars and couldn't get it out. A large student was walking by and he was strong enough that he was able to pull the bars far enough apart to permit me to remove my head. He may have been a football player as he was big and strong enough to be one. In the late forties, when the only time that they had a full stadium was for big games like the Michigan game, we used to sneak in early in the morning and hide until the game started and then grab seats usually in B deck. In those days there were dorms in the stadium. One time a student let us hide in his dorm there. Also, the OSU Theatre, which is now located in the Drake Union, had an area in the concourse part of the Horseshoe.

My cousin Herb Jones and I used to go to the OSU Natatorium and swim. We would persuade one of the students to let us in to use the pool. One day Mike Peppe, the OSU head swimming coach, saw us in the pool and he went ballistic. It was obvious that we were too young to be students and also we were the only ones wearing swim suits. He chewed out the students and threw us out. I thought he was being nasty, however in retrospect today I realize if anything would have happened to us the university would have been liable.

Herb and I used to spend our summer days swimming or fishing. We would ride our bikes over to Goodale Park and fish in the pond that they had stocked with fish. The fish were either carp or bluegills and for bait we would make dough balls out of bread. Sometimes we would fish in the Olentangy River where carp and catfish were plentiful. My dad taught me how to fish. We would go up to Shawnee Hills, just northwest of the Columbus Zoo, early on Sunday mornings and fish until noon. We also fished at Buckeye Lake, sometimes with my Uncle Oscar and Aunt Marie. One time my dad and I were fishing at Hunts Landing and I will never forget that night. We were in a rowboat and had started fishing around 8 PM and had been fishing all night. Around 1 am I was dozing off when I heard this whirring sound and I looked at my dad's reel. It was spinning so fast it was nothing but a white blur. My dad grabbed his rod and began battling this fish. When we finally got it in the boat it was a four foot channel catfish. When dad put it on his stringer and hung it overboard it kept rocking the boat. It was the only fish we caught that night but it was quite a thrill seeing dad land that big cat. I stopped fishing when I took up golf in my twenties. I should have stayed with fishing.

Getting back to what I did during the summer days of my youth, in addition to fishing my cousin Herb and I used to catch the bus and go swimming at Morningside Swimming Pool in Linden. There was a pool in Grandview on Goodale Blvd., but we didn't like that pool, so we swam every summer at Morningside when we weren't fishing. One of the other activities of my younger days was attending wrestling matches at Haft's Acre at the corner of Goodale and Park St. It was an outdoor arena where they staged wrestling matches every Wednesday night and occasionally they would offer boxing matches. My dad, my cousin Don Hansgen and I would go there. My dad would pay one dollar admission for him and 10 cents each for Don and me. The admission was ten cents for children 12 and under. My cousin and I were small for our age and we got in for 10 cents until we were 14. In September the matches would switch to Vets Memorial Hall on E. Broad St. Being young and naïve Don and I thought the bouts were real. The wrestling today on television is nothing compared to those days. Back then they had two divisions, Junior Heavyweight and Heavyweight. The Junior Heavyweights were around 175 – 185 lbs. and they were fast and actually did some wrestling. Some of the stars of those days (40s & 50s) were Johnny Demchuk, Frankie Talaber, Billy Fox, Joe Lyman, Davey Reynolds, and Billy Weidner, to name just a few. There wasn't as much showmanship as there is today. I remember that the local newspapers would publish stories on the sports pages about the upcoming bouts and then the results of those bouts the next day. Back then it was considered a sport. Today, if it appeared at all, it would probably be in the entertainment section.

Two things contributed to the demise of wrestling in Columbus, the expressway system and television. Haft's Acre was torn down to make room for the expressway system and at first the televised bouts from Chicago and New York brought new interest to wrestling but eventually led to people not attending the local bouts. For awhile they staged bouts in the summer in Reynoldsburg where Al Haft the promoter resided and owned a motel nearby. In the fall and winter months Cooper Arena on the state fairgrounds was used. The passing of Al Haft was probably the final nail in the coffin for local wrestling.

One of the men that wrestled for Haft was Dr. Bill Miller who began as "a good guy" but soon became "a villain." Miller was a veterinarian and a graduate of The Ohio State University where he wrestled and played football. Bill Miller was a Big Ten Champion heavyweight wrestler and was lineman for Coach Wes Fesler's Buckeyes from 1948 to 1950. He played on the 1949 Big Ten Co-Champion Buckeyes and in the 1950 Rose Bowl, and later that year in the infamous Snow Bowl.

I've seen a lot of changes as a lifetime resident of Columbus (I did live in Reynoldsburg from 1958 until 1965.), some good and some not so good depending on your point of view. Until about 1950, my mom and dad and I would go downtown by way of a streetcar. We lived on West Second Ave. just west of Michigan Ave. We would catch the streetcar at the corner of Second and Pennsylvania Avenues. As a youngster I was so impressed with the streetcars that I would say that when I grew up I wanted to be a streetcar motorman. I'm glad that I outgrew that fantasy. We would go downtown to shop at Lazarus, The Union, Morehouse–Martins, The Fashion, JC Penney's, The Boston Store, and Moby's department stores. HL Green, Woolworth, and Kresge five and dime stores occupied the west side of High Street from Long St. to Gay St. The five and dime stores were my favorites for buying inexpensive toys. I also loved to go to Moby's and get their malted that was similar to the present Wendy's Frosty. There were many movie theatres in the downtown area. On High Street, there were the Uptown, the Majestic, and the Knickerbocker. The Loews Broad and the RKO Palace were located on W. Broad Street. Over on State Street were the RKO Grand and Loews Ohio theatres. Next door to the Grand was the Hartman Theatre where live performances were held. One of my fondest memories was seeing the great magician Blackstone. After seeing him I now wanted to be a magician when I grew up. I purchased some magic tricks at Nelson's Magic Shop on S. High St. and would put on magic shows for the neighborhood kids on my front porch.

Speaking of movies and the theatre, there used to be movie theatres in all of the neighborhoods. In my neighborhood there was the Wilmar which was located a little less than three blocks from my house on W. Third Ave. Every Friday night my dad would give me 25 cents and my buddies and I would go to the Wilmar. For that 25 cents I would see two movies, a newsreel, cartoon, and a serial plus a box of popcorn and a candy bar. There were no multi-screens with Dolby sound, just all of the great stars of yesteryear. There was much laughter in the little theatre at the corner of an alley and Third avenue. Our Gang Comedy, The Dead End Kids, Blondie and Dagwood along with Tom & Jerry, Bugs Bunny and Elmer Fudd tickled our funny bones. It was a time of war so we saw many war movies such as *Guadalcanal Diary* with William Bendix, and Robert Taylor in *Back to Bataan*. Greer Garson and Walter Pidgeon were some of the stars that used to urge us to buy war bonds between the movies. I will never forget the story of the Sullivan Brothers. They were five brothers who all joined the Navy and none came back alive. This prompted a law that stated no family could have more than one son serving in the area of action.

I loved the serials that had a chapter once a week and the hero always was in trouble at the end. You had to come back the next week to see how it ended. *Don Winslow of the Navy*, *Dick Tracy* and *Captain Midnight* were some of the serials that I remember from those days of my youth at the Wilmar. Of course my buddies and I looked forward to the westerns. Johnny Mack Brown, Bob Steele and The Durango Kid were some of the cowboy stars of those days. Then there were the singing cowboys Gene Autry and Roy Rogers with his sidekick Gabby Hayes. Roy with his amazing horse Trigger was my favorite cowboy star. Roy would hug his horse but he never ever kissed a girl. Then one night I sat with a girl from my school and neighborhood who I thought was rather cute. In the darkness of the Wilmar theatre she gave me my first kiss and I thought "boy, Roy Rogers you don't know what you are missing."

Soon the neighborhood movie house became a thing of the past as people stayed home to watch a new phenomenon called television. That little building on the corner of the alley, which entertained young and old for many years, became a store front church of what faith I'm not sure. As a church it didn't last long and soon stood vacant and became a blighted site. Some years later in a nostalgic mood I drove by the corner of the alley where the Wilmar once stood. And it was gone. I stared at a vacant lot from my car and with sadness I realized it was gone forever, the place I so fondly remember called the Wilmar. In high school, guess who was chosen Homecoming Queen; the girl who gave me my first kiss at the Wilmar. The downtown movie theatres continued to thrive with the advent of television, but later they too vanished from the downtown scene. The only two that were saved in Columbus and are still in use are the Ohio Theatre on State St. and the Palace on Broad St. However, they are now used for live performances with the exception of the Summer Movie Series at the Ohio which continues to be popular in Columbus.

My first date with my future wife was in 1955, and it was a double date with one of my buddies, Paul Barnes and his girlfriend Marilyn Vore. We went to the RKO Palace Theatre and saw "The Girl in The Red Velvet Swing" starring Joan Collins, Ray Milland and Farley Granger. After the movie we went to Romeo's Pizzeria on W. Fifth Ave. in Grandview, a suburb of Columbus. In the early 50s this was the only pizza place in Columbus. It was owned by Romeo Sirji and Jim Massey. Later on Massey broke away and opened his own pizza place in Whitehall and then one at the corner of Cleveland Ave. and Essex. That night we had a medium pepperoni pizza for ninety cents and a couple of Cokes at five cents each. As I recall the movie was only fifty cents each. At that time I was working as a draftsman at Kinnear Mfg. for $1.26 per hour. So it's all relative. A guy by the name of Pat Orecchio, who attended the same high school that I did, opened a pizza place at the corner of NW Blvd. and First Ave. in Grandview. It was called Leonardo's and he expanded to other parts of Columbus. It is hard to believe that back then there were so few pizza joints. There were no chains like Pizza Hut, Dominoes, Donatos, and Papa Johns, etc. Today in addition to those there are many mom and pop places all over the city and surrounding areas.

Chapter 2

Byars Should Have Won And The Graveyard Of Coaches

Although my first favorite Buckeye Ollie Cline never won the Heisman, Archie Griffin and Eddie George did. Keith Byars should have won it in 1984 as he had 2,446 all purpose yards and scored 24 touchdowns and led the nation in both categories. However, when Doug Flutie completed a "hail Mary" pass to defeat Bernie Kosar and the Miami Hurricanes on national television he became the favorite for several reasons. First, Brent Musburger, the television commentator of the Boston College vs. Miami game, screamed, "Folks, you have just seen the Heisman Trophy winner," as Flutie won the game with that pass. The second reason was the quarterback position is more glamorous than the running back position. Third, he was from the east coast, which is always an advantage. Lastly, and although no one would ever admit it, he was white and there had not been any Caucasian winners since John Cappelletti of Penn State won it in 1973. Another factor was Flutie being a senior and Byars a junior, the thinking was Keith could always come back next year and win it. However, that did not materialize as Byars broke a bone in his foot just before the season opened and he never fully recovered from it. I remember Coach Earle Bruce bringing one of Keith's shoes to the Quarterback meeting and as I recall he wore a size 17 or 18. He was a big powerful back with deceptive speed and to think he was put out of action with a little bone in those big feet.

As I stated earlier, I attended my first game in the Horseshoe in 1944. Carroll Widdoes was the head coach in 1944 and 1945. He was supposed to be just the interim coach until Paul Brown returned from serving in the U.S. Navy. However, when Brown decided to cast his lot with the pros and became the head coach in Cleveland, Widdoes found himself with the job that he never really wanted. In his first year he posted a 9 and 0 record and won the conference title. He coached Ohio

State's first Heisman Trophy winner, Les Horvath, and beat Michigan. In his second year he went 7 and 2 and to this day he has the best winning percentage of all of OSU's head coaches with a 16 and 2 record and a .889 winning percentage. However, he then did something that would be unthinkable today. He switched positions with one of his assistants, Paul Bixler. Bixler lasted one season as OSU's head coach in 1946. After posting a 4-3-2 record, including an embarrassing 58 to 6 loss to Michigan, he resigned. The Buckeyes only score in that game came on a kickoff return by Rodney Swinehart. Bixler became the head coach at Colgate where there was much less pressure. In 1949 Widdoes left Ohio State to coach at Ohio University. He coached the Bobcats for nine years and his winning percentage was a respectable .599. His Ohio U Bobcats won the Mid-American Conference (MAC) title in 1953.

Former Buckeye All-American end Wes Fesler was hired as the 18th head coach of the Scarlet and Gray. Fesler was the fourth coach in seven years to take over the reins of a troubled program that was getting to be known as "The Graveyard of Coaches." That title would soon change in a few years, but that is another story.

In four years the best that Fesler could manage against "The Hated Blue" was a 7 to 7 tie in 1949. Fesler's demise came as a result of his decision to punt on third down with 47 seconds remaining in the first half of the infamous 1950 "Snow Bowl." The punt was blocked, Michigan's Tony Momsen recovered the ball in the end zone for a Michigan touchdown. (By the way, Momsen's brother, Bob, played for the Scarlet and Gray.) The point after touchdown was good for a 9 to 3 lead. This was the final score, as the near blizzard conditions resulted in a scoreless second half. In those days there weren't any letters to the sports editor on a regular basis. There wasn't any sports talk radio either. However, Russ Needham, the sports editor for the *Columbus Dispatch*, ran letters from disgruntled fans second guessing Fesler's ill-fated decision. After a month or more of this and other forms of harassment Fesler had enough and resigned.

The Snow Bowl game should have been postponed, but Michigan Athletic Director Fritz Crisler wouldn't agree to it. Michigan knew the blizzard conditions gave the Wolverines a better chance to win this game. In normal weather the Buckeyes would have beaten the Blue easily. What a shame for Vic Janowicz who kicked a 37 yard field goal into a stiff wind which would have been the winning points for a 3 to

2 baseball-type score, if the punt hadn't been blocked. The Buckeyes could have run two plays and run out the clock. Fesler's decision to punt on third down will probably go down in OSU football history as the worst decision made by a head coach.

I never saw Vic Janowicz play in person, but I will never forget listening to the play by play on radio of the 83 to 21 victory over Iowa. What an outstanding performance, as Vic had a hand in all of the scoring. Operating out of Fesler's single wing offense, he passed and ran for touchdowns. He kicked field goals, extra points and punted. Janowicz without a doubt was the most versatile and talented player to ever don the Scarlet and Gray. In 1984 I ran into Vic at the airport in St. Louis. I approached him and asked "Aren't you Vic Janowicz?" "Yes, I am," he replied with a look of satisfaction on his face. I told him that I never saw him play in person, but admired his outstanding performance in the 1950 Iowa game. He seemed pleased that I remembered that game.

I remember the Saturday of the Snow Bowl game. I was 15 at the time and a 10th grader at Central High School in Columbus. The following week schools were closed for three days and cars were stranded in the Polo Grounds all week. The Polo Grounds is where the public parked for the OSU games. It started just south of the stadium and ended at King Ave. Today that area accommodates Lincoln and Morrill Towers, several University Hospital facilities, the Franklin County Coroner's office and several parking garages. My dad and I used to walk through the grounds on Sunday afternoon after the home games as I looked for abandoned football programs. As I listened to games on the radio, I would match up the name with the pictures in the programs.

In 1949 something came to Columbus called television. In April, WLW-C channel 3 (today's WCMH channel 4) debuted, followed in the fall by WTVN (today's WSYX) channel 6 and WBNS channel 10. That year some of the OSU football games and Columbus Red Birds minor league baseball games were televised locally. That was short lived. I watched those games on a 7 inch black and white table model TV.

The thing I remember most about the 1949 season was how the Bucks lost an early season game to Minnesota 27 to 0. The game was billed as the winner would be in the driver's seat for the conference title. The Bucks won their next four games, and with a couple of upset losses by the Gophers, the Buckeyes tied Michigan for the title. Because Michigan had gone to the Rose Bowl most recently after the 1947 season, the Buckeyes were chosen to represent the conference in the Rose Bowl.

Chapter 3

That Team Up North

I have many memories of the battles with "That Team up North," some of which I attended and others I experienced via radio or TV. My first Michigan game in the Horseshoe was 1956 and the Bucks were shut out 19 to 0. Woody indicated after the game that the loss of Jimmy Roseboro hurt the Buckeye offense. Roseboro injured his shoulder while participating in the senior tackle the night before the game. After that Woody would always caution his seniors not to hit the tackling sled too hard because of what happened to Roseboro. Woody was still telling that story at senior tackle when he was no longer the head coach, but the guest speaker for Earle Bruce at the Tackle. I always looked forward to Senior Tackle and was disappointed when John Cooper discontinued opening it to the public.

The next in-person Michigan game I witnessed was the 1968 game. John Williams, a friend and a former co-worker, was given two tickets by his new employer, Jack Graf, owner of Graf and Sons Overhead Door Company. Graf played football for the Bucks and was assistant basketball coach on the 1960 National Champion Buckeyes. I remember our seats were located in the east stands where many of the Wolverine fans were also seated. The ladies were wearing roses and number 19, the number of their star running back, Ron Johnson. They were really confident that they were going to win and go to the Rose Bowl. When the score reached 42 to 14 they began to depart and some rowdy fans started shouting, "Go home and unpack your bags, you're not going to the Rose Bowl!" The Bucks were going for the first time since the 1957 season. Awaiting them was O.J. Simpson and the Southern Cal Trojans.

The next two Michigan games I watched on television. The 1969 game was a shocker when Michigan upset the heavily favored Buckeyes 24 to 12 in Ann Arbor. I had bad vibes about that game for two reasons. The first bad vibe was based on the fact that the new Wolverine coach, Glenn "Bo" Schembechler, had played for and coached under Woody. I had a gut feeling that Bo would know Woody's strategy and tendencies. The second bad vibe was based on a pre- game interview when Woody stated the Bucks would win because they had more talent. Bo replied to that by saying "No team is unbeatable." I was so depressed after the loss, that I couldn't enjoy a play that I attended that evening. It was a comedy, but I didn't laugh. My wife and all of the audience were laughing, but not me. I couldn't wait until the Michigan game the next year. All year I, and many of the Buckeye fans, had bumper stickers on our cars that read "Even on the grass, we will kick their ass!" The loss in 1969 happened on Astroturf in the Big House. The field in the Horseshoe was still natural grass, thus the meaning of the bumper sticker.

I was unable to secure tickets for the game so I was glued to the TV set as the big game unfolded. Even on television you sensed the excitement in the Horseshoe. It was a typical game between the hated rivals. The Bucks avenged the previous year's upset as they won 20 to 9.

Chapter 4

A Rebuilding Year And The Battle With Bo Continues

The next year was a rebuilding year as Kern, Tatum, Stillwagon, and all of the super sophs of '68 were gone. The Bucks new quarterback was a very talented senior named Don Lamka. However, Lamka was injured during the season and was lost for part of the year. The Bucks lost their second game after an impressive win over Iowa in the season opener. The opponent for that game was Colorado and the Bucks lost a heartbreaker 20 to 14. Late in the fourth quarter Colorado's John Stearns pinned the Buckeyes deep in their own territory with a 63 yard punt which pretty much sealed the Buffaloes victory. Stearns went on to play professional baseball for the New York Mets. In 2007, he came back to Columbus as the manager of the Columbus Clippers, a Washington Nationals minor league team at that time.

The thing I remember most about that 1971 game was how I acquired my tickets. My son Larry and I went down to the stadium in hopes of purchasing tickets from a scalper. As we heard the National Anthem being played in the stadium, we gave up and started to our car. As we walked south through the Polo Grounds three young men approached us with two tickets for sale. They only asked $10 over the face value of the tickets. I made the purchase and we ran to the stadium. When we got to our seats, I recognized that I was sitting next to State Representative Donald Woodland. As I looked around I realized we were sitting among a group of state legislators. I began to wonder where those three young guys acquired these tickets. Were they stolen? I expected at any moment some politician would show up and say we were in his seats. It never happened and we were able to see the whole game, but to this day I wonder about those tickets.

After that game the Bucks won their next five games and then proceeded to lose their final three games of the 1971 season. Michigan State, featuring running back, Eric "the flea" Allen, defeated OSU 17 to 10. The following week in conditions that started with rain and changed to freezing rain followed by snow, the Wildcats of Northwestern won 14 to 10. As this was the first year of Astroturf, the field was not affected by the miserable weather conditions. As rain was not forecast I didn't have any rain gear with me. Andy and Mary Anderson, my two good friends who gave me my ticket, let me use a blanket for protection. The blanket first got wet, then froze and then was covered with snow. Why is it that you notice the weather conditions more when your team is losing?

The next week the Bucks travelled to Ann Arbor and no one gave them a chance against the favored men of Maize and Blue. This game was not televised nationally or regionally, but instead was available on closed circuit TV. The game was shown at Mershon Auditorium on campus in Columbus. My son and I attended in a sold out auditorium. Approximately 2000 fans were screaming at a large movie screen on the Mershon stage. The Bucks played their hearts out and were leading 7 to 3 on a punt return for a TD by Tom Campana. Then the Wolverines scored to take the lead at 10 to 7. The Buckeyes had the ball and had a good drive going for a possible score. On a pass over the middle Michigan defensive back Thom Darden went over OSU tight end Dick Wakefield's back to intercept the pass. It was obvious pass interference, but the officials ruled it an interception. Woody went berserk and so did the crowd at Mershon as we shouted at the screen. Woody proceeded to tear up the sideline down markers and the official continued to walk off unsportsmanlike conduct penalties. I don't think I've ever heard the stadium crowd any louder than the crowd at Mershon that day.

The next three Michigan games were close and controversial. In 1972 the Bucks won 14 to 11 with a goal line stand reminiscent of the one in the 1954 game. Michigan only needed a tie to go to the Rose Bowl, but Mike Lantry missed a field goal at the end. In 1973 at Ann Arbor the Bucks led 10 to 0 at the half. In the second half Woody went conservative in his play calling as he tried to sit on the lead and it backfired on him. Woody refused to call a single pass play as he just kept running Archie Griffin. Unbeknownst to the fans, quarterback Corny Greene had suffered a swollen thumb on his throwing hand and instead of putting in back-up Greg Hare, Woody stuck to the ground game. Michigan, realizing that they didn't have to defend the pass played 9 to 10 men in the box. Michigan tied the score and could have won the game and the trip to Pasadena, but Mike Lantry missed two field goals late in the game.

This game and the loss in 1969 were mainly due to Woody's stubbornness. In the 1969 game it was revealed that quarterback Rex Kern had injured his shoulder and it affected his passing. Instead of bringing in Kern's back up, Woody stayed with Kern and the ground game. By bringing in Hare in the 1973 game, it could have forced Michigan to defend the pass which would have helped the running game. This would have been true in the 1969 game too. Woody was a great coach, but sometimes his stubbornness was costly.

I attended the 1974 game in Columbus. The Buckeyes could only manage four field goals by Tom Klaban but that was enough to defeat the hated Blue, 12 to 10. Once again Mike Lantry missed the kick that would have won the game and sent Michigan to the Rose Bowl. He was wide to the left. Bo said the kick would have been good in Ann Arbor, but not in Columbus. I guess he forgot that Lantry missed field goals in Ann Arbor too. The story making the rounds after the game was as follows: Lantry was so despondent after missing a game-deciding field goal for the third straight year that he took a gun out of his locker and tried to kill himself, but he missed. He was wide to the left!

In 1975 I decided to drive to Ann Arbor and try to purchase tickets from a scalper. My son Larry was a freshman at Bowling Green State University at the time. I picked him up on the way to the game. I purchased two tickets from a Michigan student at just $20 over face value. Our seats were located in the north end zone with the Michigan student body. My son and I were dressed in scarlet and gray and received much abuse before and during the game. The girl seated to my left greeted me with "F—k Woody Hayes and f—k the Bucks!" She had a jug of some sort of alcohol concoction and stated as she passed it around, "Have a drink everyone, except for these f-----g Buckeyes!" By the third quarter and Michigan leading 14 to 7 the students were so drunk they didn't know the score. In the second half I heard someone behind me gagging and vomiting and I jumped.

Luckily it was two rows back of me. The Bucks made what Woody later called, "The greatest comeback in his history of coaching," as the Bucks won 21 to 14. *Sports Illustrated* had a great two page picture of Buckeye fullback Pete Johnson scoring the winning touchdown. My wife decoupaged that picture on the top of a storage chest, and I have tried for years to secure a copy of that photo to no avail. When we departed the Big House we had to wade through empty beer cans and various other empty booze bottles in the aisle where we were seated.

The following year one of my salesmen, Bob Heinecke, and I purchased tickets from two students and they gave us their student ID's with a note stating that we were relatives. When we got to the gate they punched our tickets and never asked for the ID's. When we got to our seats in C deck we discovered that our seats were side by side but in different rows. Bob was three rows behind me. When I sat down the young man next to me asked, "Where did you get your ticket?" I told him that I purchased it from a student. He informed me that she was his girlfriend and she didn't tell him that she wasn't going to the game.

Soon the area where we were seated had more students than seats. Students were squeezed into the row and two girls came in and sat on the guy's lap to my left and one sat on the guy's lap to my right. The guy on my left started kissing the girl on his lap. I thought, wait a minute I thought he told me I was using his girlfriend's ticket. Who is this girl? Next they started passing booze around followed by what I assumed was pot. "Come on Larry, don't you want to get high?" they said to me. Watching the game became difficult as by the second half I had one girl's cheek on my left knee and the other girl's cheek on my right knee. By the end of the game, they, like the students the previous year at Michigan, were so drunk that they didn't know who was winning the game. Unfortunately the Buckeyes were shut out 22 to 0. Today some 33 years later, I wonder if those students remember that game and their wild behavior as vividly as I do; probably not. For me it was a once in a lifetime experience, whereas it was just another day at the "Shoe" for them.

The next year the Bucks travelled to Ann Arbor and once again they lost to the Maize and Blue. Trailing late in the game 14 to 6 the Bucks were driving down the field when quarterback Rod Gerald was hit and he fumbled. The Wolverines recovered the ball ending any chance the Bucks had for a victory. An ABC cameraman zoomed in on Woody just as this happened and all of a sudden you saw Woody's big paw and the next view was of the Ann Arbor sky. It was another of Woody's tantrums on nationwide television. I didn't attend the game but instead was invited by a co-worker to his house to watch the game. What I didn't know was the other guests were all Michigan fans. I had been set up. It was as bad as being at Ann Arbor. As soon as the game was over my wife and I departed. I could not bear to stay and listen to them gloat. This was the second loss to the Bucks' rival and another game when they failed to score a touchdown. I was beginning to wonder if maybe it was time for Woody to retire. Little did I know that 1978 would be the answer to that question.

Woody's Last Year!

On New Years day the men of Scarlet and Gray were humiliated 35 to 6 by Alabama in the Sugar Bowl. There was much hype leading up to this game as two football legends would be meeting for the first and only time. Woody versus Bear Bryant was a much anticipated match up. This was the beginning of a record of 0 and 9 for the Bucks in bowl games with an SEC team. As it turned out it was probably the first nail in Woody's coffin as the Ohio State head coach.

The big news that year was Woody's successful recruiting of one of the most highly rated quarterbacks in the country, Art Schlichter. Art had set all kinds of records at Miami Trace High School in Washington Court House, Ohio. There was much pre-season speculation on who would start at quarterback, senior Rod Gerald or the incoming freshman Schlichter. It was without a doubt the most closely guarded secret in Ohio State football history. No one knew until the Bucks took the field on opening day. I was at the game sitting in B deck on the west side of the stadium when both number 8 and number 10 ran out onto the field. The answer came when they broke the huddle and number 10 went under center and number 8 split out as a slot end. The Bucks were no match for highly ranked Penn State as the Nittany Lions intercepted Schlichter five times on the way to a 19 to 0 victory. This loss was followed by a tie with SMU, a loss to Purdue and for the third straight year a defeat by "the team up north." Once again the Bucks failed to score a touchdown against Michigan as they lost 14 to 3. OSU finished fourth in the Big Ten and accepted a Gator Bowl invitation where they would face the Clemson Tigers in Jacksonville, Florida on December 29.

During that season I attended the Browns game against the Pittsburgh Steelers in Cleveland with some friends. One of those friends, Don Frizzell, was a good friend of Dick Walker the defensive backfield coach with the Steelers. He knew Walker from when he was head coach at Bishop Watterson High School in Columbus. Walker later became one of Woody's assistants at Ohio State. We were to meet with Walker after the game and visit the Steelers' locker room. However, during the game Walker was injured when one of the players went out of bounds on Pittsburgh's sideline and knocked over the first down chains. One of the poles stabbed Walker in the leg and he had to be taken to the hospital. Obviously we didn't visit the locker room, which was fine with me as I'm a Browns fan. We did however go to Walker's house as was also planned. He lived in a suburb of Cleveland. When he joined us after getting stitches in his leg, we soon began talking about football. The subject of Woody came up and Walker said, "I wouldn't be surprised if this wasn't Woody's last year as head coach. I was talking to some of my former fellow coaches at OSU, and they indicated that they thought 'the old man was slipping.' The first indication was his decision to start a freshman quarterback over a returning senior. It has caused dissension on the team." He went on to say that there have been other indications of Woody showing his age.

How prophetic, as Woody lost it in the closing moments of the Gator Bowl when he punched Charlie Bauman of the Clemson Tigers which led to his dismissal as OSU's head coach. Although that has always been the stated reason for his firing, many believe as I do that if he had just not lost to Michigan for the third year in a row, he would not have been fired. I really believe that if the Bucks had won that 1976 Rose Bowl Woody would have retired and named defensive coordinator George Hill as his successor. With a second win over UCLA culminating in an undefeated season, the National Championship, Coach of the Year, and Archie's second Heisman, he could have gone out on top. Instead he stuck around three more years in pursuit of a perfect season and as a result he departed in an unpleasant manner.

Some fans tried to excuse Woody's behavior at the Gator Bowl. They said that Bauman waved the football at Woody and the players on the OSU sideline as he taunted them with the key interception. First this isn't any excuse for a head coach to punch a young man, but this didn't happen as the television replays clearly show. Bauman had his back to the bench when Woody grabbed him and turned him around and proceeded to slug him. I remember sitting in front of my TV in shock as I couldn't believe what had just happened. It took me back to January 1972 and the mugging that happened to the Buckeye basketball team in Williams Arena on the campus of Minnesota. With less than a minute to play and the Bucks leading 50 to 44 all hell broke out. Luke Witte, the Buckeye center, was flagrantly fouled by Minnesota's Clyde Turner. Witte lay on the floor and Minnesota's Corky Taylor offered a hand to help him up. Instead as he helped Witte up he proceeded to knee him in the groin. As Witte laid there in pain, Ron Behagan stomped on Witte's throat. Meanwhile Dave Winfield and some of the other players, fans and even the mascot began to attack Mark Wagar, Mark Minor, and other Buckeye players. OSU Head Coach Fred Taylor tried in vain to break up the mugging.

While all of this was happening, Bill Musselman, the head coach of the Gophers, sat on the bench with his arms folded and offered no assistance. The police had departed from the building to assist in directing traffic and were not available to help restore order. My wife and I sat there staring in disbelief at what we were witnessing on our TV. The following week *Sports Illustrated* ran an editorial criticizing Musselman, AD Paul Giel and the University for this Incident. New Big Ten Commissioner Wayne Duke suspended Taylor and Behagan for the remainder of the regular season but permitted them to play in the NCAA post season tournament. Many thought they should have been expelled from school. Duke did nothing to Winfield, which was politically motivated. Later Winfield went on to a career in major league baseball, mostly with the New York Yankees, which gave me two reasons to dislike him.

Chapter 6

From Hoops To The Gridiron!

Speaking of OSU round ball reminds me of the time when one of the Buckeye cagers decided to play football. All-American forward Dick Schnittker played for the Bucks in 1949. That team, coached by Wes Fesler, was co-champs with Michigan as stated earlier. Schnittker with his height advantage, made what was referred to as "circus catches" as he contributed to the Bucks 7-1-2 record. The next Buckeye basketball player to be a vital part of the football team was Rickey Dudley. Rickey played tight end on the '94 and '95 squads. I will never forget his clutch catch at Happy Valley that helped seal a 28 to 25 victory over the Penn State Nittany Lions in 1995. This was an especially sweet victory after losing 63 to 14 the previous year. Due to a quirk in the schedule the Bucks had to play at Penn State in back to back years. The Lions and their fans were cocksure that they would defeat the Bucks again. The only other football players that I can recall that played for the Buckeye hoopsters were Art Schlichter and Nate Salley. Both were in a reserve role. There were rumors that Rex Kern was going to play for Fred Taylor's team, but it never materialized. This according to rumors caused some friction between Taylor and Woody. It was pretty well known that Woody tried to woo John Havlicek to play football much to the irritation of Taylor. Both Kern and Havlicek were outstanding in both football and basketball in high school.

Another star basketball player in high school was Howard "Hopalong" Cassady. He never played at Ohio State but his ability in the round ball sport is what convinced Woody to offer him a scholarship in football. In 1951 Columbus East High School was the first team from the capital city to win the Class AAA High School State Basketball Championship. The following year they were undefeated heading into the Central

District final game to be played at the State Fairgrounds Coliseum. Their opponent was the Central High School Pirates, long time rivals of the East High Tigers. They were tied at the end of regulation and went into overtime. In that overtime, the Pirates were led by a scrappy little red headed guard named Howard Cassady, affectionately called "Hopalong" Cassady after William Boyd, an actor who played Hopalong Cassidy in old black and white cowboy movies. He regained popularity through his old movies that were hits on television.

Hop scored 10 points in that overtime to upset the number one ranked defending State Champion, East High Tigers. In attendance at that game was Woody Hayes and he was quoted later as saying that he thought the All State running back Hop Cassady was too small to play Big Ten football. However, watching how competitive he was in that basketball game convinced him to offer Hop an opportunity to play for the Buckeyes.

Chapter 7

"Hopalong" Cassady

In 1952, due to the Korean War that was going on at that time, the NCAA ruled that freshmen would be eligible to play on the varsity. In the opening game against the Indiana Hoosiers, Hop scored three touchdowns. That performance was the start of a brilliant career as he went on to become the Buckeyes' third Heisman Trophy winner in 1955.

I attended Central High School when Hop was playing for the Pirates. I didn't play sports as I was small for my age. When you are small you had better have outstanding athletic ability, which I didn't possess. I got most of my growth after high school. Today I'm 5'-10" 160 lbs, still not very big for playing football.

I attended all of the football and basketball games and remember some outstanding ones by Hop. He won many games for Central with his defense as well as his offensive skills. This was also true when he played for the Buckeyes. Who can ever forget his key interception in the 1954 Wisconsin game and the return of 88 yards for a touchdown which proved to be the turning point of the game? He was also instrumental in the key goal line stand in the Bucks 21 to 7 win over Michigan that same year.

In 1951 Central won the City League Championship. However, the second place team, the West High Cowboys, reported to the High School Commissioner that the Pirates had an ineligible player. Ted Alexander had transferred here from out of state and some of his credits did not count. Central had to forfeit games in which he had participated and thus West was declared the City League Champion. Assistant Head Coach Frank Howe decided to delve into West's roster and discovered that they had a tackle that had transferred here from out of state and he was declared ineligible too. The trophy was then awarded to the third place team, the East High Tigers. East said they didn't want it if they couldn't win it on the field. Rumor has it that the 1951 trophy has no name on it. By the way, the tackle who was ineligible for West was Aurelius Thomas who went on to be an All-American guard in 1957 for the Ohio State Buckeyes. And now you know the rest of the story.

Although I saw most of Hop's games in high school, I got to see him play in person at Ohio State just one time. It was in 1955 and a guy I worked with was an OSU student and working part time. He was married and his wife wasn't going to use her ticket. So I went to the game as Barbara Borror. It was Hop's final game in the Horseshoe and the opponent was the Iowa Hawkeyes. On his first carry he burst through the line behind a block by All-American guard Jim Parker and went over 40 yards for a touchdown. It was the start of a great day for the ex-Pirate as he tallied three touchdowns. His teammates carried him off the field as the game ended with the Bucks on top 20 to 10. That performance just about sealed the Heisman Trophy for the 168 lb. redhead from the west side bottoms of the capital city. The next week the Buckeyes travelled to Ann Arbor where they shut out the Wolverines 17 to 0 to clinch their second Big Ten title in a row.

Chapter 8

Penn State And Night Games

The next year, 1956, I purchased my co-worker's wife's season ticket and was able to see all of the games for the first time in my life. The game I remember the most was the first meeting with Penn State since 1912. Ohio State had started out the season with wins over Nebraska, Stanford and Illinois and was ranked fifth in the nation. The Lions were 2 and 1 and unranked. The game turned out to be a defensive battle and two costly penalties against the Bucks resulted in a 7 to 6 loss. Twice the Buckeyes were called for delay of the game as a result of late substitutions. The first came in the fourth quarter with the Bucks deep in their own territory. They were facing fourth and one for a first down. The penalty forced the Bucks to punt. A short punt enabled the Lions to start in Buckeye territory. They scored to take a 7 to 0 lead late in the game. Ohio State answered the Lions score with one of their own. When the Bucks lined up for the tying extra point, as Woody later explained, he thought he had only 10 men on the field so sent in another player. The result was a five yard penalty and Frank Kremblas' attempt was wide by inches. Penn State ran out the clock and upset the favored men of Scarlet and Gray 7 to 6. The Buckeyes would lose two more games to coach Rip Engle and the Nittany Lions before tasting victory. Today the game with the men from "Happy Valley" has become a rivalry ranking second only to Michigan.

Most of my trips to "Happy Valley" have been uneventful with the exception of the one in 2005. Whenever I travelled there on a bus with Buckeye Boosters there wasn't any of the unpleasantness that I have endured at Michigan. As we departed Beaver Stadium and headed for our bus, Lions' fans win or lose would be cordial. We would hear comments like, "nice game, have a safe trip home." However, in 2005 we were greeted with "the Bucks s—k, f—k the Bucks, and overrated." They bumped us and threw mud balls at our bus. Before the game they attacked our band as it was leaving Bryce-Jordan Center. They threw urine on the band members, mooned them and stole the plumes from their hats, and accompanied it with foul language. I think it was brought on by the frustration of losing three straight games to the Bucks and after several losing seasons they just didn't know how to handle success. Probably the main factor that contributed to this kind of behavior was the fact that it was a night game to accommodate television. That gave the fans all day to get liquored up. We ran into a similar situation at a night game at Wisconsin in 2003. I dislike games played at night. College games should be played on Saturday afternoon at 1:30 PM, outdoors, on natural grass.

The Wisconsin trip was made through Travel Pals instead of Buckeye Boosters. The rain held off long enough to enable us to tailgate. We parked in a lot behind McDonald's on the Wisconsin campus. While tailgating we were visited by John Ivanich, news anchor, and Dave Maetzold, sports director, of Channel 4 in Columbus. While using the men's room in McDonald's I ran into Tom Hamilton, the radio voice of the Cleveland Indians. I told him that I was a long time Indians fan and he was the best announcer since Jimmy Dudley. He seemed to appreciate the compliment. It started out to be a great trip, good food and drinks at the tailgate and meeting some TV and radio celebrities. Then it started to rain and it poured all through the game with the exception of late in the fourth quarter.

The Bucks 19 game winning streak was halted by the fired up Badgers by a score of 17 to 10. Chris Gamble got burned on a long pass to Lee Evans for the winning touchdown. Earlier Gamble fumbled a punt that set up another Badger score. Instead of falling on the fumble Gamble kept trying to pick it up and failed. During the game the Bucks defensive end Robert Reynolds was penalized for choking the Wisconsin quarterback in a pile up. A fan seated behind us had a small portable TV and after they showed the incident on television, he really started letting us have it, calling the Buckeyes dirty players, etc. After the game the students went wild and started taunting the Buckeye fans. Unfortunately we had to walk through the campus bar area to get to our bus. They were in our face saying the Bucks were dirty players and the Bucks were overrated. After being told this numerous times I finally said to one very drunk student; "If the Bucks are overrated, why are you so happy about defeating them?" That seemed to shut him up.

I remember fondly the days when we defeated the Badgers by blow out scores and the students didn't mind and they just partied. This is just another example of what happens at night games and fans not being able to handle success. I will say that the night game at Northwestern in 2004 did not produce those results. Although it was a big upset and the first time since 1971 that Northwestern defeated the Bucks, the fans celebrated but were not repulsive. This was my first time to attend a game at Evanston and except for the outcome of the game we had a nice visit in Chicago. Northwestern's Ryan Field was the only Big Ten stadium which I had not previously visited in person.

Chapter 9

The Fiasco At East Lansing

One of the road trips I made was very memorable for different reasons. It was on November 9th 1974 and the place was East Lansing, Michigan. The Buckeyes were ranked number one in the nation with a record of 8 and 0. I drove to East Lansing and accompanying me were two of my customers and one of my fellow salesmen. The trip up was uneventful and we were confident that we would be 9 and 0 at the end of the day. Little did we know what was ahead of us. As any true Buckeye knows, the end of the game was controversial. Did Ohio State score before time ran out or did time run out before they scored? In my opinion the officials did a poor job of officiating in the last seconds of that game. The Spartan players deliberately prevented the Buckeye players from getting up and back to the line of scrimmage on the last play, including one player holding Buckeye center Steve Myers down by the face mask. The officials should have called an officials time out when they observed the Spartan players holding the Buckeye players down. As a result one official ruled a touchdown and another indicated that time had expired before the play was run. It was around 45 minutes after the game ended before Big Ten Commissioner Wayne Duke ruled the Spartans the winner 16 to 13. I can still close my eyes and see Levi Jackson running right at us, as we were seated in the end zone, with a big smile on his face as he outran Neal Colzie to the end zone. That was the score that put MSU in the lead 16 to 13.

We were waiting in our seats at the top of the end zone bleachers for a decision to be made about the game, when some rowdy Spartan students carried a portion of the goal posts up there. I overheard one of them say, "If they take this game away from us we're going to drop this on anyone wearing scarlet and gray." I told the guys with me that I thought we had better get out of there before things got ugly.

We were in our car and down the road several miles before we heard Duke's ruling. I was not surprised that Duke ruled the way he did, after the way he handled the mugging of our basketball team at Minnesota in 1972. As we travelled back to Columbus we continued to replay the game. It certainly looked like Champ Henson had scored. But the officials ruled that he was stopped on about the half yard line. If they had ruled that a touchdown the game would have been over without the next controversial play. Why didn't the officials give the Bucks the opportunity to run that last play, etc?

We decided to stop at an L & K restaurant in Bowling Green, Ohio. I noticed that my gas gauge showed nearly empty. I thought that I would fill it up at the Sohio station next to the L & K after we had eaten. One of my customers, Bob Johnson, was from Mt. Vernon, Ohio, and there happened to be some friends from there in the restaurant. He decided to ride with them back to Mt. Vernon, thus saving me the trip. As we headed south on Rt. 23 my engine began to sputter about 10 miles north of Marion, OH. Right away I realized that I had forgotten to get gasoline back in Bowling Green. I pulled over to the berm. We were out in the middle of nowhere. I noticed a farm house east of the road with lights on in the house. I hiked over there and I could see a gasoline pump back near the barn. I knocked on the door but they refused to answer, so I headed back to the car.

When I got back I started thumbing and many cars passed me by without stopping. Finally one car stopped and offered me a ride into town so I could get some gas. It was a young couple from Zanesville, Ohio, and they had been to the game. They said the only reason they stopped was because I was wearing my Ohio State scarlet and gray clothes. When we got to the Sohio station at the first exit to Marion, the attendant was alone and could not take me back to my car. He sold me a can of gasoline, and the young couple offered to take me back, which I thought was very kind of them. They not only took me back, but waited to make sure my car started. I tried to pay them for their efforts on my behalf, but they refused to take any money. That year, 1974, I ran out of gas three times. I had been driving since 1952 and had never run out of gas and I have not run out of gas since the last time in 1974 on my trip home from East Lansing.

The Bucks went on to win the remainder of their games and were Big Ten co-champions and headed to the Rose Bowl. Their opponent would be the Southern California Trojans for the third year in a row. This would be the rubber match with the Bucks winning last year and the Trojans prevailing the previous year.

Chapter 10

My First Rose Bowl

This was my first of three trips to Pasadena. My wife and I travelled with the Barker – Bradford Travel Agency. We were excited about this trip as the package included a trip to Disneyland, Universal Studios, and Hollywood, etc. We packed our bags, including swim wear and sun screen, as we were headed for sunny California. When we left Port Columbus it was 32 degrees with snow flurries and when we landed in Los Angeles it was 40 degrees and raining. This was typical of the weather the whole time we were there. In fact, on the morning of the Rose Parade the weatherman was forecasting 30 degrees with the possibility of snow. It didn't snow but it was very cold. We were seated in the bleachers for the parade and we watched the people on the other side of the street shed their coats and sweaters when the sun came out. We were in the shade and never had the benefit of the warm sun. It did get up to 60 degrees at kickoff that day, but became very chilly when the sun went down late in the game.

Prior to the game we had a less than satisfying experience with the various attractions we were eager to see. We were on a Circle Line bus tour which picked us up at our hotel in downtown LA. Our trip that day to Disneyland was a disaster. The bus dropped us off at 10 am and informed us we had to be back at the bus by noon. We had tickets for five attractions. After standing in line for two of them we ran out of time to see the other three. As we were making our way back to the bus I saw some OSU cheerleaders entering the park and I gave them our three remaining tickets. The same thing happened at Universal Studios. We had two hours to see all of those attractions. Needless to say we didn't get to see much. These two incidents were bad enough, however the worst was yet to come. The driver of the bus told us to be back to the bus in 45 minutes when we departed the bus at Grauman's Chinese Theatre. My wife and I looked at all of the famous stars footprints and hand prints in concrete that are in front of the theatre. I took some pictures. After 30 minutes I noticed that our bus was leaving without us. We ran to the bus and as it was pulling away I pounded on the door and the driver stopped and let us on. I gave him a piece of my mind and he lamely claimed that he thought everyone was back on the bus. I informed him a competent bus driver would have done a head count before and after every stop. He was a frustrated wanna-be entertainer driving a bus.

We finally got to see sunny California on New Year's Day. The Rose Bowl is in a beautiful setting. Our seats were located on the east side of the stadium, row 72 on the 20 yard line. The Grand Marshal for the Rose Bowl was Henry Aaron who had just broken Babe Ruth's all time home run record of 714 that past baseball season.

As we were watching the bands and all of the pre-game festivities, three couples came in and sat right in front us. I couldn't believe my eyes as they were all decked out in Maize and Blue Michigan outfits. I tapped on the shoulder of the guy in front of me and asked him why they were here. He informed me that they had purchased a package deal for the game prior to the OSU and U of M game. They were certain that Michigan would prevail so they purchased the Rose Bowl package and decided to go even though the Wolverines wouldn't be playing in the game. I asked who they would be rooting for and they said the Big Ten even though it was the Buckeyes. I always take my boat horn to the games and blow it when the Bucks enter the field and for touchdowns, fumble recoveries, interceptions, etc. The first time I blew it one of the women in front of me was startled. I apologized and told her I would aim it up in the air instead of directly behind her head. As the game progressed it became obvious that the group from that state up north were actually cheering for USC. Guess where I started blowing my boat horn after I discovered that? The Bucks lost that game to the Trojans 18 to 17 on a late fourth quarter touchdown pass from Pat Haden to coach John McKay's son and a two point conversion to flanker Shelton Diggs. With time running out the Bucks' Tom Skladany tried a 62 yard field goal that fell just short. I was ready to blow my horn as the kick was as straight as an arrow but fell short of the cross bar into the arms of USC player. More about this and other games in my chapter entitled "If only."

The traffic leaving the game was horrendous and as a result we missed watching on TV the entire Orange Bowl game between Notre Dame and Alabama. As it turned out, Notre Dame upset the number one ranked Alabama. If the Bucks had won the Rose Bowl they would have been number one. Instead Oklahoma was crowned number one by AP and USC by UPI.

Chapter 11

Trips to Ann Arbor

My trips to Ann Arbor with the Buckeye Boosters have been a mixture of memories, some good, some not so good. It was 1981 and my second trip to The Big House and the first with the Boosters. The Bucks were trailing late in the game 9 to 7 when quarterback Art Schlichter rolled right on an option as three U of M players closed in on him. However, between Art and the Wolverines was OSU fullback Vaughn Broadnax. He threw a block into the first defender and proceeded to wipe out all three of them. They fell like pins in a bowling alley. It was the prettiest block I have ever seen executed. Schlichter walked into the end zone as the Bucks won 14 to 9. Suddenly it didn't seem as cold and dreary in the Big House for those of us decked out in scarlet and gray.

On the trip home we stopped at the Inverness Country Club in Toledo, Ohio for dinner. After a delicious steak dinner we boarded the buses for the final leg of our journey back to Columbus. One of the Booster officers got on our bus and informed us that someone had taken a very expensive ceramic ashtray from the dining room. We would not be leaving until it was returned. My wife Marty and I felt very uncomfortable. As the newcomers on the trip we were afraid that we might be suspected of the theft. Finally someone returned the item and we were able to depart.

Our next trips to Michigan were in 1983 and 1985 and they were both forgettable losses. However, the trip in 1987 was a very memorable one as it was Earle Bruce's last game as head coach of the Buckeyes. He had been fired earlier in the week and I was very sad, as were a lot of Buckeye fans. I'll never forget how the Buckeye players all wore head bands with the inscription "Earle." The team was really pumped up for the game and it was great to see them upset the favored Wolverines. Our seats as usual were terrible. We were down very low with the band in front of us and the Buckeye bench to our left. Any action that took place directly in front of us and to our right we could see. We were on about the five yard line and any action from there that was near the sideline and headed to our left was blocked by the players on the sideline. When Carlos Snow caught a pass in the flat that he turned into a 70 yard touchdown that put the Bucks up 14 to 13, we could not see him after he caught the pass. The seats that OSU allots to U of M fans are considerably better than what Michigan gives the Buckeye faithful. You are really scrunched in there with your knees in the back of the person in front of you, and the person behind you with their knees in your back. It is no wonder they can seat so many in their stadium. The Bucks won the game when Matt Frantz put three on the board late in the game to clinch the 23 to 20 win. He made up for the field goal he missed the previous year which cost the Bucks the game. As we were leaving the stadium, the Michigan fans yelled at us, "You should be ashamed of yourselves for firing your coach!" I told several of them I agreed with their comment.

Earle vs. Cooper

I will always believe Earle's firing in 1987 was political and was dictated by the movers and shakers of downtown Columbus. It was not coincidental that he was fired the same year that Woody died. I believe that Woody protected Earle from the downtown crowd. When Earle came to Columbus he discovered that Woody was being underpaid for his TV show. All of the big time coaches, like Bo, Bear, Joe Pa, and Lou Holtz were getting paid six figures for their TV shows. Woody of course, never being interested in money was being paid a rumored four figures. It was recommended by other coaches to Earle that he should produce the show himself and put it out for bids. He did and channel 4 had the winning bid and for the first time in 26 years the show wasn't on channel 10. Channel 10 was owned by the owners of the local newspaper and they had a good deal of power in the city. So that was the first nail in Earle's coffin. Earle also didn't live football 24/7 as he was a devoted family man. Therefore he didn't go to all of the parties and hob nob with the high rollers and benefactors of the university. That was another nail in his coffin, and along with the factor that the OSU President didn't like Earle, he was doomed. With Woody no longer around to protect him it was curtains for the coach who at the time had the best winning percentage of any coach in the Big Ten. He defeated Michigan five out of nine times and the four losses were close games. That is more than could be said about his successor. The coach who succeeded Earle was John Cooper. The reason given for the hiring of Cooper was he could take the Buckeyes to the next level, an undefeated season and the national championship. Earle had earned the nickname of "old 9 and 3 Earle."

If this good old boy from Tennessee could do this that would be fine with me. However, I noticed that in his years at Arizona State he never defeated their arch rival Arizona. Even the year that he won the Pac 10 and defeated Michigan in the Rose Bowl he lost to Arizona. I saw this as a bad omen. Everyone who didn't like Bruce was talking about how Cooper defeated Michigan. My reaction to that was so what? That doesn't prove anything. Bo Schembechler had a terrible bowl record. Just look at Cooper's record in the rivalry games. If he can't win the Michigan game there won't be any undefeated seasons and national championships. Thirteen years later I was proven correct in that regard.

Speaking of Bo, I've never understood his being considered one of the great coaches in college football. Look at his record, he never had an undefeated season, never won a national championship and had a miserable bowl record. He did win the ten year war with Woody (5-4-1) but other than that what did he accomplish to be considered with the likes of Woody, Bear Bryant, Paterno, Wilkinson, Osborne, etc.

Getting back to Cooper, the other thing that bothered me about him was his statement in his first season about the cupboard being bare. I could see right through that ploy. In my profession as a sales manager I was familiar with this kind of statement. When one of my fellow managers would be promoted to another branch office they would make the same kind of statement. "Boy, what a mess I inherited. I will have difficulty making quota this year." In this ploy the manager is covering his "you know what." If he doesn't make quota it wasn't his fault and if he makes or exceeds quota, what a fantastic job he did. This is why I figured we had ourselves a "slick talking, southern snake oil salesman," as our new head football coach.

The next 13 years were some of the worst years and some of the most disappointing years in the history of Buckeye football. Cooper is the only head coach at Ohio State to have two six loss seasons. His first year of course was because the cupboard was supposedly bare. However, the other six loss season in 1999 was with his recruits. In addition to being the only OSU coach to lose four in a row to Michigan he also had a losing record in bowl games and against Illinois. Keith Byars, a former OSU running back (82-85) was quoted as saying "being 0 and 4 against Michigan is bad enough, but being 0 and 5 versus

Illinois is unbelievable." Cooper's bowl record was 3 and 8, including a very humiliating loss to Air Force in the 1990 Liberty Bowl. The Cooper apologists would say that this loss proved that the cupboard was bare. My answer to that would be, what about the blowout losses to Michigan 31 to 3 (1991), 28 to 0 (1993), and Penn State 63 to 14 (1994)?

I will say this, that Cooper did provide this long time Buckeye fan with some moments I will always treasure. His two outstanding wins over Notre Dame and his come from behind wins at Minnesota and Iowa and in his first year against LSU in the Horseshoe were great. The 1997 Rose Bowl win over Arizona State was one of his greatest victories. He also posted a winning record against Joe Pa and the Penn State Nittany Lions (5-3). However, he had one of the worst butt kickings in OSU history in the aforementioned 1994 loss at Happy Valley.

I found Cooper's Quarterback Club meetings in his first years to be not as interesting and informative as Earle Bruce's had been. All we heard were his little sayings that we had heard all week via the media. For example, "one week you're drinking the wine and the next week you're stomping the grapes." "I was born at night, but not last night." After about thirty minutes the meeting was over. Earle's meetings lasted at least an hour and sometimes longer. Earle brought players to the meetings and would get very animated in describing plays. Later on Cooper began bringing players and he showed film of the opponents and answered questions, etc. I will say one thing about Cooper. He was very friendly and approachable after the meetings, as was Earle.

Today I cannot say that about Coach Vest (Jim Tressel). He comes in with Dick Smith on one side and Steve Snapp or someone else on the other side like bodyguards and he leaves the same way. He is without a doubt an outstanding coach and worth every dollar the university is paying him, but he is very aloof. However, I will take his record over the team up north and his aloofness over his predecessor's record and friendliness any day.

Chapter 13

"What If"

Modern day football is considered to have begun in 1936. It was at that time that the national championship was determined by the Associated Press (AP) poll of sports writers. The United Press International (UPI) was determined by the coaches. Prior to 1936 there were various organizations that selected the national champions. Today the champions are determined by the Bowl Championship Series (BCS) and the AP. They usually agree. However in 2003 they didn't, as LSU and USC shared the title. From 1936 until the advent of the BCS, most schools were recognized by either the AP or the UPI polls.

In looking at the polls since 1936 the schools with the most national championships are Alabama with nine and Notre Dame with eight. Oklahoma and USC each have seven national titles. Ohio State, Miami and Nebraska each have five. Minnesota and Texas each have four. LSU and Florida are tied with three each. In the fourteen years of the BCS, Alabama, Florida and LSU lead with two BCS titles. Ohio State has two additional titles: one in 1961 by the Football Writers Association of America (FWAA), and in 1970 by the National Football Foundation (NFF). However, the ones that really count are the AP, UPI and the BCS.

All of this got me to thinking how if only this or if only that had happened, how many championships would the Buckeyes have today? When I add these up the Bucks would be leading the nation with 18 titles.

Return with me to 1961. The Buckeyes, after a disappointing tie with Texas Christian, ran off eight straight victories including a pounding of Michigan 50 to 20 in Ann Arbor. However, since the invitation to play in the Rose Bowl was extended to The Ohio State University rather than the Athletic Department, the decision to accept the invitation rested with the Faculty Council. Led by Jack Fullen, Secretary of the Ohio State Alumni Association, the invitation was rejected. I was in shock as were all Buckeye fans. Woody was livid. Fans marched down High St. from the campus to the State Capital in protest, but the decision stood. Minnesota, the second place team, was invited and accepted. As a result of this decision the Bucks season was over and they finished 8-0-1 and second to Alabama in the final poll. Alabama won their bowl game. The Big Ten made certain this could never happen again, but it was too late for the undefeated Bucks of 1961. If only the Faculty Council had voted to accept the invitation the Bucks would have played UCLA in the Rose Bowl. Minnesota defeated the Bruins 21 to 7. Although OSU didn't play Minnesota that season I feel certain the Bucks would have won. If only ... if only ...

After winning the National Championship in 1968 with a sophomore laden team the Bucks were heavy favorites to successfully defend their title in 1969. Being hailed as the best team of the century the Bucks headed to Ann Arbor to play their hated rival Michigan. Having humiliated the Maize and Blue (50 to 14) the previous year the Bucks were favored. This Buckeye team was considered to be even better due to the year of experience of the Super Sophs - Kern, Tatum, Stillwagon, Brockington, White, etc.

Michigan had a new head coach, Bo Schembechler, who had played for Woody at Miami of Ohio and was an assistant coach at Ohio State under Hayes. As I stated previously in this book, I had vibes about this game. I could almost feel an upset coming although on paper it didn't seem possible. Unfortunately, quarterback Rex Kern was not 100% for the game. Kern's back up Ron Maciejowski was capable of leading this team, and would probably be the starter on any other team in the Big Ten. But, Woody decided to go with Rex, and the result was a stunning 24 to 12 upset. I still to this day cannot believe this explosive offense only scored 12 points. It is obvious that Woody just got out coached. Michigan went to the Rose Bowl, and the Bucks stayed home and watched TV. If you lose a game and expect to be National Champions, you had better lose early in the season, not the last game. Alas, Texas was named number one. If only Woody had started Maciejowski. If only the Big Ten permitted teams to play in other bowls, as they do today, a big bowl victory might have given the Buckeyes the National Title. If only … If only …

In 1970 with the Super Sophs now being seniors, the Buckeyes rolled through their schedule and once again found themselves ranked No. 1. as they approached their final game of the regular season. The Bucks got their revenge with a convincing 20 to 9 win over that "team up north." The Bucks were headed to the Rose Bowl. Their opponent was Stanford, a team with a 6 and 3 record, but featuring the Heisman Trophy winner, quarterback Jim Plunkett.

The Bucks were leading in the game 14 to 10 in the fourth quarter and faced a fourth and one on Stanford's 19 yard line. They failed to get the first down, and Plunkett took over and drove Stanford 80 yards to a go ahead score. Another score sealed a 27 to 17 upset victory of the number one Buckeyes. Little Randy Vataha made several sensational catches of Plunkett's passes to help put the Buckeyes away.

Ohio State with the great sophomores of '68 once again was thwarted in their quest for No. 1 by losing the last game of the season. Nebraska would be crowned number one. This great OSU team would finish their careers with a three year record of 27-2-0. What looked like a certain three straight National Titles in 1968 ended with one title and two heartbreaking misses.

Many would compare their fate with that of the great OSU basketball teams of the early 60s with Lucas, Havlicek, and Nowell. They won the NCAA Title as sophomores, only to lose in the final game to Cincinnati in their junior and senior years. If only the Bucks had made that first down on fourth and one. If only Randy Vataha hadn't made that unbelievable catch. If only … If only …

1971 and 1972 were off years, although in 1972 the Bucks did beat Michigan and go to the Rose Bowl. They were thrashed by a powerful USC team featuring "Bam Bam" Sam Cunningham, 42 to 17. USC was named National Champions. A bright spot in that season was a young freshman from Columbus Eastmoor High School, Archie Griffin. The future looked bright and rosy!

1973 saw the Buckeyes go undefeated and once again ranked number one, as they approached their annual showdown with the Wolverines in the Big House. The Bucks moved to a 10 to 0 lead at the half. Coach Hayes buttoned up the offense in the second half and depended on his defense to protect the 10 – 0 lead. This strategy backfired, and Michigan fought back to tie the game. The next day the Athletic Directors voted to send the Bucks to the Rose Bowl, much to the chagrin of Bo. The Buckeyes responded by demolishing the defending National Champion Trojans of Southern California, 42 to 21. The next day Notre Dame was named No. 1 and once again the men of Scarlet and Gray were denied the National Crown by one game. This time the only blemish on their record was a tie. What if Woody had opened up the offense instead of sitting on the lead? What if? ... What if?

1974 was the first of two Heisman Trophy years for Archie Griffin, and the Bucks rolled into East Lansing to face the Michigan State Spartans. The Bucks were undefeated and ranked number one in the nation. This game ended on a controversial note, as the officials denied the Buckeyes a last second touchdown and the Spartans prevailed 16 to 13. Alabama replaced Ohio State as No. 1 the next week. What if the officials had allowed the touchdown? What if the officials had called an officials time out? This would not have been unusual, as it was obvious that the Spartans were deliberately not allowing the Buckeye players to get up. There was no way the Buckeye players could get back to the line of scrimmage where the ball rested one foot from the goal line. What if? ... What if?

Despite this setback the Bucks went on to win their remaining games, including a 12 to 10 thriller in the horseshoe over Michigan. The Bucks were Rose Bowl bound for the third straight year and a rubber match with the Trojans of Southern Cal. If Notre Dame could knock off Alabama in the Orange Bowl, and the Bucks defeat the Trojans, No. 1 was still a possibility.

OSU led 17 to 10 late in the game, and Neal Colzie intercepted a Pat Haden aerial and returned it to the USC 10 yard line. Instead of handing the ball to the official, the exuberant Colzie spiked the football. The official threw the flag—15 yards for unsportsmanlike conduct—and instead of first and ten just outside the 10 yard line; it was first and 25, just outside the 25 yard line. The Bucks never scored. Later Pat Haden hooked up with J.K. McKay on a long bomb and it was now 17 to 16. The Trojans went for two and the lead. Arnie Jones, the rugged Buckeye nose guard, came close to sacking Haden, but Haden was able to loft a pass in the end zone to flanker Shelton Diggs. It was now 18 to 17 in favor of the Trojans with less than two minutes remaining in the game. OSU drove to mid-field, and Tom Skladany tried a 62 yard field goal that was right on line but fell just short of the cross bar.

Notre Dame did their part as they upset No. 1 Alabama in the Orange Bowl. But once again, No. 1 slipped through the Bucks fingers, as Oklahoma was named number one in the AP poll and Southern Cal in the UPI poll. If only Colzie hadn't spiked the ball, if only Arnie Jones had sacked Haden. If only Skladany's kick had been a yard longer. If only … .If only.

With a backfield composed of Corny Greene, Brian Baschnagel, Pete Johnson and Archie Griffin, Ohio State finished the 1975 regular season undefeated and ranked number one in the country. Archie won his second Heisman Trophy, Pete Johnson was the leading scorer in the nation, and Corny Greene was voted the MVP of the Big Ten. After the thrilling come-from-behind win over Michigan in Ann Arbor the Buckeyes appeared ready to claim their first national title in 7 years.

The Buckeyes were headed to the Rose Bowl for the fourth year in a row. This time their opponent would be the Bruins of UCLA. The Bucks would have preferred Southern Cal to avenge last year's heartbreaking loss. UCLA tied California for the PAC 10 title and the Bruins had defeated the Bears in their head to head meeting; therefore UCLA won the right to represent the PAC 10 in the Rose Bowl. The men of the Scarlet and Gray had already defeated the Bruins 41 to 20 early in the regular season at the Los Angeles Coliseum. It is always difficult to defeat a team twice in the same season. The Buckeyes were a 15 point favorite and the Buckeye fans were confident that the Bucks would prevail and end their two-game losing streak in the Rose Bowl. I wasn't as confident as the so-called experts and most of the Buckeye nation. I remembered that the Bucks led 28 to 0 at half time in their earlier encounter. However, the Bruins out-scored the Bucks in the second half 20 to 13. Did UCLA's coaching staff make some adjustments at half time to their offense and defense to make them play more competitively with OSU, and there just wasn't enough time remaining and the deficit was too big to make up in that first game? Would the second meeting be a different story? Would the Bucks be over confident?

The Bucks ran and passed at will against the Bruins in the first half, just as they had in their previous meeting. The difference this time was they only had 3 points to show for it. OSU won all of the statistics in the first half, first downs, yardage, time of possession, etc., but UCLA only trailed 3 to 0 at half time. The second half was all UCLA, as they out-scored the Bucks 23 to 7. In the fourth quarter the Bucks were trailing 16 to 10 when Craig Cassady, son of Hop Cassady, intercepted a pass. On the first play, Greene under threw a pass to Lenny Willis and it was intercepted inside the UCLA's 15 yard line and retuned for almost 15 yards. The Bucks held and forced the Bruins to punt. Greene was intercepted again. This time Wendell Tyler burned the proud Buckeye defense on a 54 yard run for a game-clinching TD. A very sad and dejected Woody Hayes made his way across the field to shake hands with the young Bruin's coach, Dick Vermeil. Once again, Oklahoma, despite an early season loss was named No. 1. What if Corny Greene had not under-thrown Lenny Willis in the fourth quarter? What if OSU had played Cal instead of UCLA? What if the Bucks hadn't played UCLA in the regular season? What if?... What if?

It's now 1979 and for the first time in 28 years there's a new head coach directing the men of Scarlet and Gray. After Woody's firing there was a big push by the fans for OSU to hire Lou Holtz. When Earle Bruce was announced as the new coach the reaction was: "Who in the hell is Earle Bruce?" This was similar to the reaction back in 1951 when Woody was announced as the new head coach. "Who in the hell is Wayne Woodrow Hayes?" At that time there was a big push to "Bring back Paul Brown!"

No one expected much from the team that was 7-4-1 the previous year. In addition, their All-American linebacker Tom Cousineau was gone. However, with a more versatile offense and career years from guys like offensive tackle Tim Burke, middle guard Tim Sawicki, and outside linebacker Jim Laughlin, the Bucks won their opener and kept on winning. Quarterback Art Schlichter was outstanding as the Bucks took to the air more, with Art hooking up with receivers Doug Donley and Gary Williams. A big win in the finale at Ann Arbor preserved an undefeated regular season, and a Big 10 championship and a trip to the Rose Bowl made believers of those who questioned the hiring of Bruce.

In the Rose Bowl the Buckeyes would face a strong Southern Cal team, featuring Heisman Trophy winner Charles White and All-American offensive tackle Anthony Muñoz. The Bucks trailed 10 to 0, but came back to tie the score at half time. This reminded me of the 1969 Rose Bowl when Rex Kern and the super sophs trailed USC by that same score and came back to tie the game just before the half. Late in the fourth quarter, the Bucks drove deep into USC's territory and were faced with a third and short, leading by the slim margin of three points 13 to 10. They failed to make the first down and settled for a field goal. I was beginning to anticipate the first victory in the Rose Bowl in six years with a National Championship as the icing on the cake. With less than 3 minutes to play, the Trojans began a long drive, featuring Charles White behind the blocking of big Anthony Muñoz. Ohio State's outstanding defensive tackle, Luther Henson, was injured and did not play in the game. His back-up, Gary Dulin, played his heart out for over three quarters, but behind the blocking of Muñoz, and White's running of the infamous student body right, Dulin wore down. With just seconds to play, White scored, the PAT was good, and time ran out on the Buckeyes. USC 17, OSU 16. Another season with one costly loss, and Alabama was named National Champions. If only Gary Dulin could have hung in a little longer. If only Art Schlichter hadn't been stopped on the one yard line on fourth and goal; if only ... If only.

That would prove to be Coach Earle Bruce's only shot at a national championship in his nine seasons as The Ohio State University football coach. His successor at the helm for the next 13 seasons had four opportunities at winning the national title. However, once again we had four what ifs or if onlys.

In 1993 the Buckeyes were once tied but undefeated heading into their annual showdown with arch rival Michigan. The week before the Michigan game they defeated Indiana at the horseshoe. At the end of the game several players mugged for the TV cameras with a rose clenched between their teeth and holding up their index finger indicating they were number one. Alas this would come back to haunt them. Michigan players saw this celebration after the game and were quoted as saying this was a factor in motivating them for their game with the Bucks. When the Michigan players were gathered at the tunnel leading to the field they observed some of the Buckeye fans wearing roses. Ty Wheatley, running back for the Blue, told some of the Buckeye faithful that if the Bucks won the game he would come back and eat those roses. It was obvious that the Buckeye players and fans were overconfident going into this game. After Michigan shut down the Buckeye offense on their way to a 28 to 0 victory, the players were quoted as saying, "When we saw the Buckeye players celebrating on TV after the Indiana game we thought, you are not going to the Rose Bowl and be number one until you come to our house and defeat us." To this day I do not understand why Coach Cooper permitted that kind of behavior from his players. His lack of discipline would prove to be his undoing in the future.

The Buckeyes were 6-0-1 going into that game and Michigan was 4-3 in the conference. As a result the Buckeyes ended the regular season tied with Wisconsin at 6-1-1. The Badgers received the Rose Bowl bid. The tie breaker was the third option, who had gone to the Rose Bowl more recently. What if the Buckeyes had not celebrated prematurely on national TV, maybe the Wolverines would not have been so motivated for this game ... what if?? Wisconsin won their game with UCLA in the Rose Bowl and the Bucks won their game with BYU in the Holiday Bowl. However, Florida State was declared the 1993 National Champions with a record of 11-1. Florida State's loss came early in the season. If the Bucks had beaten Michigan they would have finished the season 11-0-1 and undoubtedly would have been named number one. The loss to Michigan cost them an outright Big Ten title, a trip to the Rose Bowl and a possible national championship. If only ...

The Buckeyes were not in contention for the national championship in 1994. However, they did defeat Michigan, giving Cooper his first win over the hated Blue.

The year 1995 saw the Bucks roll through their non-conference schedule and the first seven games of the Big Ten undefeated. They were favored in their season ending match with the Wolverines in Ann Arbor. However, Tim Biakabutuka, Michigan tailback, ran for 313 yards as the underdog Wolverines prevailed 31 to 23. The Buckeye defense could not stop Biakabutuka's cut back runs and the 12th ranked Wolverines upset the favored number-one Buckeyes. As a result of Biakabutuka's performance, he was drafted eighth in the first round of the 1996 NFL draft. The week after that game I attended WTVN radio's Bucks Line at the Scoreboard restaurant in Columbus. I asked Earle Bruce how you defend the cut back runs that were so successful for Michigan in that game. He said, and I quote, "You have one of your linebackers stay home and not pursue the runner." Why didn't the coaches make that adjustment? Once again a loss to the hated Blue cost the Bucks the Big Ten title, as Northwestern won the crown, and another possible shot at the national title. If only the Bucks coaching staff could have made the necessary adjustment and stopped Biakabutuka, the Buckeyes could have finished the regular season undefeated. They would have gone to the Rose Bowl as Big Ten Champions and with a victory there, could have possibly been national champions. If only ...

As it turned out the Bucks went to the Citrus Bowl where they lost to number four Tennessee 20 to 14. This seemed to be a pattern for the Bucks under Cooper. When they lost the Michigan game they usually followed that with a loss in the bowl game.

The only exception to that pattern was the 1996 season. Once again the Bucks were undefeated heading into their annual battle with that team up north. The number one ranked Buckeyes were favored over the 21st ranked Wolverines. The game was being played at the Horseshoe in Columbus and not even the most die hard Michigan fan thought the Blue would prevail in this clash. Their one hope was John Cooper's record in this rivalry. I was so confident that the Bucks would finally finish their season undefeated by coming out on top against the hated Blue. I was really pumped for this game and before the game I attended the "skull session" at St. John Arena. This basketball arena was packed with noisy Buckeye fans and a sizeable number of Wolverine fans. I happened to be seated next to a Michigan fan and when their band began to play, he leaned over and said to me, "Now you're going to hear a real band." I noticed that all of their band members had music on their instruments, so I shot back, "Oh it's too bad they can't memorize their music like the OSU band members do."

In the first half the Buckeyes drove inside the Wolverines ten yard line three times, but had to settle for three field goals. The score at the half was OSU 9 Michigan 0. This was not good and it reminded me of the 1976 Rose Bowl. In that contest the Buckeyes drove up and down the field and racked up first downs and yardage but only led 3 to 0 at the half. They ended up being upset by the UCLA Bruins which cost them the National Championship. Could this be an omen?

In the second half the Wolverines kicked two field goals to make the score 9 to 6 in favor of the Bucks. On third down Tai Streets caught a pass over the middle for a possible first down. However, cornerback Shawn Springs slipped when trying for the tackle and Streets went all the way for a touchdown. A pass that was thrown for a first down went instead for a TD and the Blue were now leading 13 to 9.

Earlier in the game, flanker Dimitrious Stanley was wide open as he had the only defender beaten by ten yards, but OSU quarterback Stanley Jackson overthrew him by ten yards. So once again the Bucks season was ruined by an inferior Michigan team as the Wolverines held on to win 13 to 9. Ohio State was co-champions with Northwestern, instead of outright champions, but they did go on to play in the Rose Bowl. Not only couldn't Cooper's teams beat Michigan they also couldn't win an outright Big Ten Championship.

The Buckeyes did win a come-from- behind thriller in the Rose Bowl as they defeated Pac 10 champion Arizona State. The Bucks finished the season 11-1 and second to the Florida Gators for the National Championship. The Gators also finished with an identical record of 11-1, but their loss came earlier in the season. Once again, if you are going to lose you had better lose early in the season.

If only Shawn Springs hadn't slipped. If only Jackson hadn't overthrown Stanley. If only the Bucks could have scored one touchdown in the first half instead of three field goals. If only ... If only ...

In 1997 the Bucks had a chance to do to Michigan what they had done to the Buckeyes in '93, '95 and '96: beat them and thus deny them an undefeated season and a shot at the National Championship. They failed, as the Wolverines won 20 to 14. Stanley Jackson was intercepted twice in a game where OSU won the battle of statistics, but lost the war. Cooper's use of two quarterbacks, Jackson and Germaine, was about as successful as his use of Bob Hoying and Bret Powers in '93. I always felt that if he had played Germaine instead of Jackson in '96 and '97 we would have won those Michigan games. If only ... If only ...

In all of the pre-season polls the Buckeyes were ranked number one heading into the 1998 season. They opened with the number 11th ranked Mountaineers of West Virginia at Morgantown, West Virginia. My wife and I and two other couples drove down to Morgantown to the hotel where the Buckeye Boosters were staying. The West Virginia fans were confident that they were going to pull off the big upset over the favored Buckeyes. We travelled by bus with the Boosters from their hotel to the stadium. The traffic was horrendous, but was mild compared to what we faced after the game. There were signs everywhere poking fun at Andy Katzenmoyer due to the article that had appeared in the latest edition of *Sports Illustrated*. In that article it was revealed that Katzenmoyer was taking golf, music appreciation, and Aids awareness. We met an old friend, Kacy Bunner, and had lunch with him at a cafeteria across the street from the stadium. Kacy, a fan of the Mountaineers, was confident that the Bucks would be unable to stop their star running back, Amos Zereoue. Well, the Bucks did and they won 34 to 17. Our bus was parked in a ravine with only one exit. The game was one of those scheduled to accommodate TV, an 8 PM kickoff. The game was over around 11:30 PM but we didn't get out of the parking lot until 1 AM. Our car was back at the Boosters' hotel. We had accommodations at a motel in Ohio near St. Clairsville. We had estimated that the game would be over around 11:30 and we would be on the road by midnight. We had guaranteed our rooms for late arrival. It was a good thing we did, because instead of checking in around 1:30 am we arrived around 3:30 am. I really hate those late night games. As Earle Bruce always said, "College football games should be played at 1:30 on a Saturday afternoon, outside, and on natural grass."

The Buckeyes continued to be ranked number one as they defeated the 21st ranked Missouri Tigers and the number 7th ranked Nittany Lions of Penn State. The men of Scarlet and Gray looked unbeatable as they out-scored their opponents 306 to 72. That other team from the state up north, the Michigan State Spartans, came to Columbus on November 7th to play the Bucks in the Horseshoe. OSU was a heavy favorite over a team they had defeated the previous year 37 to 13 in East Lansing. It looked like another victory as the Bucks led 24 to 7 late in the third quarter. The Spartans scored the next 21 unanswered points and upset the number one team 28 to 24. One of the key plays in the game which set up one of the Spartan scores was as a result of a freak occurrence. MSU had punted to the Bucks and the ball took a strange bounce and ricocheted off Nate Clements' leg. The Spartans fell on the ball and recovered it deep in OSU's territory. The Buckeyes still had a chance to pull out the win as they drove to the Spartan 15 yard line late in the fourth quarter. With first and ten at the fifteen Joe Germaine threw four passes into the end zone and the last one was intercepted. That sealed the victory for the green and white. Why didn't the Bucks try at least one running play or a pass over the middle to the tight end, or a screen pass to Michael Wiley?

The large crowd of scarlet and gray clad fans sat stunned as the few thousand fans in green and white stormed the field in wild celebration. As I sat there in disbelief I harkened back to 1974 when Levi Jackson and the officials upset the number one Buckeyes. In both of these losses the better and much more talented team had their hopes for a National Championship crushed.

If only that ball hadn't ricocheted off Clements leg ... if only ... if only ... If only the Bucks had run the ball or thrown a pass over the middle to the tight end or thrown a screen pass to the back out of the backfield ... if only ... if only ...

I'm convinced, if the Bucks won that game, and it was winnable, they would have defeated Tennessee in the first BCS National Championship game.

If only? ... if only? ...

The next "if only" game was the 2007 BCS National Championship game in Glendale Arizona. The Bucks' previous trips to Arizona resulted in three victories. The Bucks were favored and with the Heisman Trophy winner at quarterback and receivers like Ted Ginn, Jr. and Anthony Gonzalez the Buckeyes could score quick and often. The Florida fans were very confident as they kept giving us the Alligator Chop. I returned that with a gesture like a hook in a fish's mouth.

When Ted Ginn returned the opening kickoff for a touchdown the Buckeye crowd went nuts. I yelled to the Florida fans, "Where's that SEC speed now?" Unfortunately Ginn was injured during the touchdown celebration and was out for the game, something we fans in the stands didn't realize at that time. Although the Gators defeated the Bucks decisively, I believe losing Ginn changed the game for the Gators defensively and the Bucks offensively. Urban Meyer, the Florida coach, commented after the game that having Ginn out of the game made their defensive plans easier. "We didn't have to double team him which made Gonzalez a threat. With Ted Ginn in the game you have to know where he is all of the time," commented Meyer.

With Ginn out of the game it not only hurt the Buckeyes passing game, but it also took away the reverse and even the "Shot-Ginn" we saw in the 2004 Alamo Bowl. I also couldn't believe that Coach Tressel went for the first down on fourth down deep in their own territory. That was very un-Tressel like. What was even more puzzling is when he had Troy Smith rolling out to pass deep in the Buckeyes territory which led to a fumble. Trailing 23 to 10 late in the first half, I thought Tressel would run the ball, take time off the clock, and punt. Instead of going in at the half down by 13, the Bucks trailed by 20. A very difficult mountain to climb, which they never did. If only Ginn had not been injured and lost for the game ... if only? ... if only Tressel hadn't gone for it on fourth down ... if only?... if only Tressel had played it more conservative just before the half ... if only?

The most recent "if only" came in the 2008 BCS National Championship game. The Buckeyes were a very controversial number one and their opponent climbed over several other teams to be an equally controversial number two. It was the LSU Tigers versus the Buckeyes as both were pursuing their second BCS title. Once again the Buckeyes struck first with a big run by tailback Beanie Wells giving the Bucks a 7 to 0 lead. Later the Bucks had a chance to take the lead but Brian Robiskie dropped a touchdown pass in the end zone. In the second half, the Buckeyes forced LSU to punt and the Bucks went for the block and missed it by mere inches. Instead of blocking the punt and getting great field position, the Bucks were penalized for roughing the kicker. If only? If Robiskie doesn't drop the pass in the end zone? if only ? If only that punt could have been blocked. If only? ... If only?

Sum up the entire if onlys and what ifs and the Buckeyes would have 18 National Championships. All the other schools would trail the men of Scarlet and Gray. But, also it would mean Texas, Notre Dame, USC, Florida, Alabama, LSU, Oklahoma, and Nebraska would have fewer national crowns.

If only? ... if only? ...

Chapter 14

Other Bowl Games and Trips

Some of the other bowl games that I attended were the 1984 Fiesta Bowl, the 1990 Hall of Fame Bowl, the 1993 Citrus Bowl, the 1993 Holiday Bowl and the 1998 Sugar Bowl.

The 1984 Fiesta Bowl at the time was not one of the big New Year's Day bowl games. The big four were the Rose, Orange, Sugar and Cotton Bowls. The Fiesta Bowl was played on January 2nd in Sun Devil Stadium, home of Arizona State. We looked forward to our trip with the Buckeye Boosters as my wife's former sister-in-law lived in Phoenix, and we hadn't seen her in years. We travelled from Columbus to Phoenix via Windwalkers, a private charter line. It was quite an adventure. The stewardesses appeared to be TWA rejects. As we approached the airport in Phoenix, water began to come into the plane from the ceiling. The stewardess instructed us to hold our pillows and blankets up to the ceiling, explaining that this was normal, as condensation forms when you descend from high altitudes. I told one of the stewardesses' that I had been flying for many years and I had never experienced anything like this. When we hit the runway the plane bounced several times, the overhead compartment doors came open and the contents began to fall out. The pilot's name was Cheetah and all I could think of was the chimp in the Tarzan movies.

The next day we decided to go for a swim in the hotel outdoor pool. It was heated and it was 77 degrees and sunny that day. It was very pleasant and felt a lot warmer than the temperature, probably because we were used to the temperatures back in Ohio. That evening when Tina, my wife's ex sister-in-law, picked us up to go out to dinner, she was wearing a winter coat, with gloves and a scarf. It was 55 degrees and she was shocked to hear that we had gone swimming earlier that day. I guess when your body is used to 110 degrees and higher, when it gets in the 50s to 70s range it feels like our 30s in Ohio.

The next day we took a bus trip to Flagstaff and the Grand Canyon. The bus picked us up at 6:30 am and then made several stops to pick up more people. The bus then dropped us off at the Hyatt in downtown Phoenix at 7:15 am where we were to wait for the bus to take us to the Grand Canyon. That bus would arrive at 8 am. Because we had to be ready so early we didn't have time for breakfast, so we decided to have some breakfast at the Hyatt. Boy, was that a mistake. I had a bowl of oatmeal and orange juice and my wife had two slices of toast and juice. The bill was close to twelve dollars and this was in 1983!

On the way to the Grand Canyon we noticed that one of the passengers was a young man who was blind. I thought this was strange, a blind man on a sightseeing trip. Our seats on the bus were in front of the rest room at the rear of the bus. This young blind man went into the rest room and we couldn't help but overhear him as he was engaged in a violent argument with someone. We didn't see anyone go in the restroom with him and when he exited no one else came out. It was obvious that he had other problems in addition to his blindness.

As we got near Flagstaff we noticed that there was snow on the ground and when we exited the bus we discovered the temperature had dropped too. The bus parked near the edge of the Canyon near a gift shop. We exited the bus to take some pictures and visit the gift shop. When we returned to the bus we were startled to find the young blind man seated in the driver's seat and fooling around with the controls. This was scary because of where the bus was parked. Much to everyone's relief the driver took over and the young blind man returned to his seat.

The weather was nice for the game and it was an exciting one, as the Buckeyes came from behind to defeat Pittsburgh 28 to 23. Trailing late in the fourth quarter 23 to 21 everyone thought that the Bucks would go for a field goal to win the game. With 39 seconds left on the clock, quarterback Mike Tomczak hit split end Thad Jemison for a 39 yd. TD. Jemison was named the MVP for the game, tying a Fiesta Bowl record with his eight catches. This was a big surprise as Jemison had been an ineffective receiver who seemed to have concrete hands. Jemison finished his career at Ohio State with his best game ever with his eight catches totaling 131 yards and scoring the winning touchdown.

The trip home was uneventful and a victory always makes the trip home shorter. Little did we know that the next time we would be in Phoenix we would win a double overtime thriller to become the BCS National Champions.

Speaking of that game, I know there are some Miami Hurricane fans and those around the country that dislike the Buckeyes, who feel that Miami lost because of a controversial call. It was only controversial because the official was late in making it. It was without a doubt the correct call as not only was Miami guilty of pass interference but they also committed holding several times on that play. The picture in the Arizona Republic the next morning clearly shows Chris Gamble being held in the end zone. I remember the Miami team clearing the bench and running out on the field and they started to roll out the platform for the trophy presentation, when I noticed a flag in the end zone. I yelled to devastated OSU fans around me, "There's a flag! There's a flag!" All that did was give the Bucks another shot at the end zone and Miami failed to stop the Buckeyes. When OSU scored in the second overtime, Miami had a chance to score and tie the game, but they failed. In my judgment, and replays of the game confirm my opinion, the game should never have gone into overtime. Ohio State should have won 17 to 14 in regulation. The game replay clearly shows that Michael Jenkins caught the ball inbounds and then went out of bounds. The completion would have given the Bucks a first down. It was ruled incomplete and the Bucks had to punt. Miami had a long return of the punt and that set up the tying field goal that sent the game into overtime.

I'm looking forward to the 2010 season when those Miami Hurricanes come to the Horseshoe to play the Buckeyes for the first time since that BCS Championship in 2003. Their only other trip to Columbus came in 1977. The Bucks prevailed in that season opener 10-0. That was prior to the Hurricanes becoming a national power.

The 1990 Hall of Fame Bowl had the Buckeyes facing the Auburn Tigers in Tampa. I have never experienced such cocky, arrogant fans as those Tiger supporters. It just made me want the Bucks to defeat them the way they did the LSU Tigers in 1988. That game was Cooper's first year and it was the third game of the season. After a convincing win over Syracuse in the home opener the Bucks got their butts kicked in Pittsburgh by the Panthers. The previous year, Earle Bruce's last year, the game ended in a 13 to 13 tie in Baton Rouge. The Bucks should have won that game, but the officials had other ideas as they made some controversial calls, being intimidated by the rowdy LSU fans in the "Snake Pit." As Ohio State lined up to try a game winning field goal late in the fourth quarter, the official suddenly moved the spot back about a yard from where it had originally been spotted after the last play. The kicker, Matt Frantz, had already paced off his approach and the change led to him missing the three pointer.

In the 1988 rematch in Columbus the Bucks trailed by 33 to 20 with a little over four minutes to play in the game. The Buckeyes rallied to score 16 points and pull off the upset. The Tiger fans that were seated four or five rows behind me had been taunting the Buckeye faithful all during the game with their little song and yelling "Tiger Bait." As they departed with their "tiger tails" between their legs we really let them have it. Unfortunately our spirits were crushed the next week when the Bucks were soundly beaten by Illinois and then by Indiana and Purdue. Cooper ended up 4-6-1 in his first season and in his next to last season he posted a 6-6 record to have the dubious honor of being the only Ohio State head coach to have two six-loss seasons.

Getting back to the bowl game in Tampa, it was the Bucks first appearance in a bowl game in two years. The men of Scarlet and Gray led 14 to 3 late in the first half. However, with just seconds remaining in the half, Auburn scored to cut the margin to four points at the half. Auburn dominated the second half and went on to hand the Buckeyes their first of the eight bowl losses under Cooper.

My wife and I didn't go with the Buckeye Boosters on this trip. We put a trip together on our own. I had accumulated enough frequent flyer miles that I was able to get our air fare free. A friend from our church, Loran Miracle, owned a travel agency and was able to get us a good rate on a rental car. I booked rooms at the Hampton Inn about five minutes from the stadium. Jimmy Crum, Sports Anchor for WCMH – TV 4 in Columbus was also staying at that hotel. We saw Jimmy and his wife and the crew from TV 4 several times and chatted with them during our stay. I was on the committee with Jimmy when John Johnson and his organization "Try Love" did a salute to Woody Hayes about a year before he passed away. I later served on that same committee that honored Jimmy Crum the next year.

We had a good time during our stay in Tampa leading up to the game. We visited the old restored part of Tampa and spent a day at Busch Gardens. On New Year's Eve we found a quaint German restaurant that had a delicious buffet and an oom-pah band that helped us bring in the New Year. We stayed over after the game and visited my wife's mother who lived in Jensen Beach, Florida. We had heard that Disney World's crowds were smaller after the holidays and we found this to be true as we spent a day there.

We didn't attend the Liberty Bowl in 1990 and I was glad we decided to stay home as it was embarrassing enough watching it on television. The underdog Air Force Falcons upset the Bucks in one of the most miserable performances by the Buckeyes I have ever witnessed. After three seasons under Cooper the Buckeyes had lost three straight to Michigan and Illinois, and two bowl games.

In 1991, after losing our fourth in a row to Illinois and Michigan, we lost in another bowl game that I did not attend. This time it was to Syracuse in the Hall of Fame Bowl in Tampa. What I remember most about that season was the butt kicking that was administered to the Bucks by the hated Blue. To this day ABC TV, during highlights of past college seasons, will show Desmond Howard in his Heisman Trophy pose in the Bucks end zone. Shortly before the noon kickoff, the president of Ohio State announced that he had just extended Cooper's contract for four more years. When John Cooper arrived at Ohio State he stated that the cupboard was bare and that he had inherited too many "slow white guys." If this was true why did the Bucks play better with those "slow white guys" against Michigan than this year when most of the team were now his recruits? In 1988 OSU lost 34 to 31, in 1989 28 to 18, and in 1990 16 to 13. In 1991 the Bucks lost 31 to 3.

The Buckeyes opened the 1992 season with two close wins at home. The opponents were the Louisville Cardinals and the Bowling Green Falcons. Both were close games as the Bucks eked out a one point win over Louisville and a 17 to 6 win over BGSU of the Mid-American Conference. There are two things I remember about these games. During the Louisville game our large defensive tackle, Alonzo Spellman, sacked the Cardinal quarterback and when he got up he went along the Louisville sideline taunting the Cardinal bench. I was surprised that the officials didn't throw a flag for unsportsmanlike conduct. I was even more surprised that our head coach didn't pull him out of the game and get in his face. This kind of conduct would prove years later to be typical of Cooper-coached teams. In the Bowling Green game my wife and I wore a mixture of Buckeye and BG clothing. Our son graduated from Bowling Green and we found ourselves rooting for both teams; my wife more so than me.

The third game of the '92 season was a rematch of the 1992 Hall of Fame Bowl in which the Orangemen of Syracuse defeated the men of Scarlet and Gray 24 to 17. This time the Bucks had to travel to New York and face Syracuse at their home field in the Carrier Dome. My wife and I and our friends Ted and Sally Messner travelled with the Buckeye Boosters for this game. Prior to the game we enjoyed side trips, including a visit to the Baseball Hall of Fame in Cooperstown. My family had visited Cooperstown in 1968 and I was looking forward to another visit to this historic site. My wife did not want to visit there again as she and my daughter were bored stiff on the last trip. However, my son and I really enjoyed the visit and reliving the history of baseball.

The previous trip in 1968 was our first stop on our way to Cape Cod. We often travelled without getting motel reservations in advance and never encountered a problem finding a vacancy. When we arrived in Utica we thought we would either get a motel in Utica or drive down to Cooperstown and get one closer to our destination. As we travelled south from Utica we didn't see any nice motels. There were rooms for rent above stores, etc. but nothing at all appealing for a family traveling with a seven year old daughter and an eleven year old son. When we arrived in Cooperstown the only place to stay was a large hotel that was way too expensive for my budget. So we decided to go back to Utica and get a place there. The first motel indicated they had one vacancy and after agreeing on a price, we unloaded our luggage. We climbed the stairs, found the room and opened the door, only to find the room already occupied. After getting my money refunded and giving the manager a piece of my mind we loaded our luggage back in the car and finally located a nice motel. Just before we checked in, I stopped to fill up my tank at a nearby service station. While doing this a guy came up to me and asked me, "How's work back in Ohio?" After exchanging a few pleasantries, he asked where we were headed and when I told him he stated, "Oh, there are all kinds of nice places to stay on the way down there." Oh yeah, I thought if you don't mind staying in "Flora's Flop House." When I told him we had found a place just up the road he said, "Oh that place, they've had a lot of murders there recently." Needless to say we didn't sleep too easily that night. I don't know why it is, but no matter where we travel, I always seem to attract the characters.

As we continued on our way to the Cape we stopped in Amityville, Long Island, NY, to visit with my wife's aunt Ginny Flesche and her daughter Helen Campbell and her family. We were going to stay at a nearby motel, but Aunt Ginny insisted that we stay with her. That evening she made lasagna for dinner and it was absolutely delicious. The next night we had a nice visit with the Campbell's. Then the next morning it was off to the Cape.

The week before we departed I had taken my car in for service at Krieger Ford in Columbus. The alternator light kept coming on and then it would go off. The service department assured me that it was probably just a defective bulb and it was safe to travel. From Columbus to Cape Cod it would come on and then go off, so I just ignored it. However, when we got just outside of Hyannis Port the light came on and stayed on. The car began to act as if it was going to stall, so I exited and just barely made it to a service station. The man at the service station indicated that it was something that the local Ford dealer would have to handle. The dealer was closed for the day. We had to get a room in Hyannis Port and the cost of the room was not in my budget. As we walked around the town looking for a place to eat, it was obvious there weren't any fast food places there. We ended up eating in a Chinese restaurant and that wasn't in my budget either. I had a restless nights' sleep as I worried about what the repair of my car would cost. The next day the service manager at the Ford dealer indicated that he was too busy with local customers to have time for tourists. He said that he would look at one thing and hope that was the problem. In about a minute he said it was fixed. He said there was a wire that wasn't making contact and it was draining my battery. He attached it and charged my battery and, best of all, there was no charge as the car was still under warranty. He indicated that he could not understand why the people at Krieger Ford didn't discover this and I wondered too. I definitely would pay a visit to Krieger when I got home. The rest of the trip was without incident as we enjoyed the beauty of Cape Cod and had our first taste of fresh lobster.

Meanwhile, back to 1992 and our next visit to the Baseball Hall of Fame in Cooperstown. It was a long bus trip from Syracuse, approximately 3 hours one way, and they only gave us 2 hours to tour the facility. I was really upset about this as we had spent a whole day there on our last visit and still did not see everything. To add insult to injury our tour guide on the bus was a big Syracuse fan and we had to listen to him on the way over and back about how the Orangemen were going to really kick the Buckeyes' butts. Finally when we returned to our hotel we told him to stop by after the game and we would buy him a drink regardless of the outcome of the game.

The big mouthed Syracuse fan never showed up at the hotel after the game because the Buckeyes defeated the eighth ranked Orangemen 35 to 12. Senior quarterback Kirk Herbstreit opened the game with a long bomb to split-end Brian Stablein to go up 7 to 0. The partisan orange clad crowd sat in silence. Freshman Eddie George scored three touchdowns as the Scarlet and Gray avenged their earlier defeat that year.

The next week the Buckeyes jumped from number 21 to number 12 in the national rankings. That was short lived, as the Bucks were upset by Wisconsin in the Horseshoe. Next was a heartbreaking loss to Illinois which was also a home game. Illinois players bragged that they owned the Horseshoe. They had earned that bragging right when the Bucks lost to them for the fifth year in a row with three of them coming in the 'Shoe! In that game Eddie George, who would go on to win the Heisman Trophy in 1995, had two crucial fumbles. The first fumble occurred as he was going in for a touchdown. Instead Illinois recovered and went over ninety yards the other way to score. Later in the game George fumbled inside Illinois' five yard line which prevented the Bucks from scoring. They lost 18 to 16 and the Bucks dropped to number 21 in the polls.

The Buckeyes had lost five in a row to Illinois and four in a row to the Maize and Blue. Would they lose their fifth in a row to the hated team up north? The answer was no, as they, according to Gordon "Mr. Bow Tie" Gee recorded their "greatest victory ever," in a 13 to 13 tie. It was a game they could have very easily won, but alas it didn't happen. Sometimes it seemed as though John Cooper was snake bitten as he never got a break in this annual rivalry. Late in the fourth quarter with the score tied OSU punted to Michigan. The Michigan player signaled for a fair catch and he fumbled it. If the Bucks had recovered the ball they could have at least kicked a field goal and won the game. But, no, Michigan recovered the fumble and ran out the clock. Later the player who recovered the fumbled punt stated that he had started up field to block on the return, but out of the corner of his eye he saw the signal for a fair catch and he stayed back and the ball bounced right to him.

After finishing the regular season 8-2-1 the Buckeyes accepted a bid to the Citrus Bowl in Orlando, Fla. Their opponent would be Georgia from the SEC. In previous bowl games with the SEC the Bucks were 0-2, losing to Alabama and Auburn. The eighth ranked Bulldogs featured All–American running back Garrison Hearst. The fifteenth ranked Buckeyes also had a good running back in Robert Smith. With the score tied at 14 and the Bucks driving for a go ahead score there was a fumble of a handoff in the backfield, and the Bulldogs recovered inside their own twenty. The Buckeyes were now 0-3 versus the SEC, which would eventually go to 0-9 by 2008.

Although we didn't get to see the Bucks take home a win, we did have a good time. We travelled to the game with our good friends the Messners and the Buckeye Boosters. We stayed at the Holiday Inn in Melbourne, Florida. Prior to attending the game, we enjoyed some other activities during our stay. We had a rental car and one day we decided to travel north to the Kennedy Space Center. Marty, my wife, and I with our son and daughter had visited the space center in the seventies, and a lot had changed since that visit. On the morning we were to depart I was watching the weather forecast for the area on television. The meteorologist indicated that although the morning was cloudy and chilly, it would be sunny and in the mid-sixties by noon. Based on this forecast, I decided to wear shorts and a golf shirt. When we met the Messners in the lobby they were dressed like my wife for the day to remain cloudy and chilly. They questioned the way I was dressed, but I told them it was going to get warmer. Well, it didn't! It never got warmer than 40 degrees and with the wind blowing and no sun I almost froze. At the space center most everything is outside and my teeth began to chatter. We cut the visit short due to my stupidity. We came back a few days later when it was sunny and warm and thoroughly enjoyed the tour of the center.

On another day, Ted suggested that we go to the dog races. Marty and I had never been to the dog races and she wasn't too keen on the idea, but we decided to go. I'm not much of a gambler, but I decided to place a bet or two just for the fun of it. I hit on something called a trifecta for $120. It is where you pick three dogs to finish win, show, and place. I wanted to keep betting but Marty said no that I should quit while I was ahead. I heeded her advice and only picked the rest of the races but didn't bet any money. As it turned out I selected several more winners and could have won a good deal more than the $120. For the rest of the trip when I would start to spend money, Marty would question me on this, and I would tell her that I was just "spending my dog money."

One funny incident happened concerning one of the other Buckeye Boosters. Art Chamberlain, a long-time member, did a favor for Ted, and Ted wanted to show his appreciation so Art said, "Oh, just buy me a screwdriver sometime this week." Ted, not being a drinker, didn't know what Art was talking about. I suggested that we go to the local Wal-Mart and buy him a screw driver in their hardware department. You should have seen the look on Art's face when Ted thanked him and handed him that screw driver.

On New Year's Eve, the Boosters had a dinner dance at our hotel and we celebrated the end of 1992 which for me was an especially difficult year. The company I had worked for since 1966 was sold to Océ, a Dutch company. This was upsetting and unexpected and I didn't know what the future held for me. However, the most devastating experience in 1992 was the death of my mother. She had been feeling ill for several months and the doctor finally decided that she needed her gall bladder removed. Before this happened, I got a call from my dad around 5 am on September 29th and we rushed my mom to the emergency room at Riverside Hospital in Columbus. They scheduled her for gall bladder surgery the next day. However, during the surgery they discovered she had inoperable liver cancer. She was referred to Hospice and given three to six months to live. Mom was 80 years old and had been in good health other than the usual aches and pains of old age. Unfortunately mom was a bit of a hypochondriac and we were never sure when she really was sick. On November 6th she passed away just 19 days short of her 81st birthday. The year before I had a surprise 80th birthday party for her at Schmidt's German restaurant in Columbus. A lot of family and friends gathered in their party room for dinner. I was so glad that I did that as her last birthday was a special one for her and all of us. We didn't know at the time it would be her last.

Our next bowl trip with the Boosters was the next season when we travelled to San Diego for the Holiday Bowl. After being tied 14 to 14 by the Badgers in Madison, Wisconsin the Bucks still had a shot at the National Championship. All that stood in our way was "That Team up North." With a win over Michigan the Buckeyes would finish the regular season 9-0-1. The Bucks were favored in this game even though they were playing in Ann Arbor and the Bucks were 0-4-1 under Coach John Cooper and had lost two in a row at the "Big House." Coming into this game Michigan had lost four games. The Bucks were led by All-Americans Korey Stringer on the offensive line and Big Daddy Wilkinson on the defensive line. The Bucks were poised for their first victory in Ann Arbor since Earle Bruce's last year in 1987. It didn't happen, as they were humiliated 28 to 0. John Cooper was quoted after the game, "If I had known we were going to get beaten 28 to 0, I would have stayed home." That was the last time that I attended a game in Ann Arbor and I too wished I had stayed home. On the way out of the stadium we were greeted by the fans clad in maize and blue with taunts of "overrated, overrated!" As we headed for our bus, a guy they call Officer Mike taunted us over his microphone with, "Goodbye Buckeyes see you in two years and bring John back, we love John up here." Two drunken students got on our bus and sang "Hail to the Victors" and a bunch of rowdy students started to rock our bus. I said to my son, Larry, who had accompanied me to the game, "I'm never coming back here again," and I have not. After a disappointing end to the 1993 regular season it was good to be headed West, even though it was not to Pasadena.

The Holiday Bowl was not a New Year's Day bowl as it was played on December 30th. The Buckeyes would be facing the same opponent they played on their last trip to the Holiday Bowl in 1982. They would be clashing with Brigham Young. The 9-0-1 Buckeyes were heavy favorites over the 6-5 Cougars. Early in the game it looked as though the Buckeyes might repeat their 47 to 17 win in their last Holiday Bowl encounter with BYU, as the Bucks jumped to a 21 to 7 lead. However, the Cougars roared back with two scores and the game was tied at half time. Ohio State was driving with the ball and appeared to be on their way to improve their lead to 28 to 7 due to the powerful running of Raymont Harris. Then on a third down and short play Harris was taken out and Butler By'not'e was put in the game. He failed to get the first down and the Bucks had to punt. I believe that had Harris stayed in the game the Bucks would have scored and the rout would have been on. Why take a power running back out when BYU couldn't stop him, and put in a smaller quicker back and try running him up the gut? That is one of many coaching decisions that Cooper made that I never understood. In the end the Bucks just barely pulled out a victory 28 to 21, as the Cougars drove deep into the Bucks territory three times in the fourth quarter but failed to score. At last Cooper had his first of only three bowl game wins in his 13 years as the Buckeye head coach. A dismal record topped only by his horrendous record against Michigan.

We had a good time in San Diego and we fell in love with this city. My friend Ted Messner and I agreed of all the locations of the bowl trips we had taken, we found San Diego to be a place that we would like to live. The weather was perfect with beautiful blue skies and mild 70 degree weather. The natives told us that they don't get much rain, just enough to keep things from drying out.

When we go on these Boosters' trips we always rent a car and this was no exception. This time we rented from Thrifty Car Rental. They came to our hotel and picked Ted and me up and took us back to their car lot. While there Ted was discussing the rental car with the agent and he turned to me and said, "Do you want a Buick or Chevy?" I wasn't paying attention and replied," Huh?" So Ted proceeded to raise his voice and asked me again. I told him it didn't matter and to get whichever he wanted. But, from that moment on every time the agent would talk to me he would raise his voice. "WILL YOU BE DRIVING TOO, MR. HANSGEN?" "CAN I SEE YOUR DRIVERS LICENSE, MR. HANSGEN?" At the time it wasn't funny, but now we still laugh about that situation when we are recalling some of our trips with the Boosters.

Another incident on this trip wasn't funny at the time, but now we find it amusing. We took a trip to Sea World and after a fun time there we were getting ready to exit the parking lot and I thought everyone was in the car. So I started to pull away and just then Sally, Ted's wife, yelled for me to stop as she was half in and half out of the back seat of the car.

While we were in San Diego, Marty called her younger brother Richard who lived in nearby El Cajon. We met him for lunch at a Fuddruckers one day and then made arrangements to go to his home later where we met his wife and children. They had a beautiful home located in a canyon and we had a nice visit. We also got to meet all of their cats. Attached to one side of their house they had a building which housed twenty plus cats of all varieties. His wife, Marge, is a cat lover and had taken in many strays. It was good that it was not part of their house as the odor was very unpleasant.

The day before the game they had a Holiday Bowl parade and we attended that with Richard and his family. It was a good parade with floats and bands, etc. It is nothing like the Rose Parade, but still a good one. Of course we all cheered when the OSU marching band and the cheerleaders came by.

Down the street from our hotel there was an impressive white cathedral which really stood out against the beautiful clear blue sky. We thought we would go down and see if we could see the interior. We discovered it was a Mormon cathedral and it was only used for baptisms and weddings. Furthermore, only Mormons are permitted inside. We were made aware of this in the nearby gift shop where we were very subtly urged to convert to the Mormon faith.

We also walked on the beach of the Hotel Del Coronado in San Diego where the movie "Some Like it Hot" was filmed. It is a very large and beautiful beach with pure white sand and on that day had a backdrop of a blue cloudless sky. Another interesting site was Mission San Diego, the first church founded in California in 1769. It was a small white church with very lovely flower gardens surrounding it.

On the day of the game we met one of my former sales reps, Connie Burkett, for a short visit prior to the game. She had transferred to the Los Angeles branch earlier that year. She was really enjoying living in California, although it is considerably more expensive than Toledo Ohio, her former residence.

All in all it was a great trip topped off by a Buckeye victory which was in doubt right down to the last play of the game.

1994 was not a good year for the Bucks who went 9 and 4 overall and 6 and 2 in the conference. Once again they lost to Illinois in the Horseshoe for the fourth straight year under Cooper as they fell to 1 and 6 against the Fightin' Illini. They were humiliated by Penn State 63 to 14 in Happy Valley and they lost a road game to Washington. Marty and I, accompanied by the Messners, went with the Buckeye Boosters to this game, which was the second game of the '94 season. After defeating the number 12th ranked Huskies at night in the Horseshoe the previous year we were confident as we travelled west to face the 25th ranked Huskies. Coming off a convincing 34 to 10 win over Fresno State in the Disneyland Pigskin Classic to open the 1994 season the Bucks looked more than ready for their encounter in Seattle.

On our flight out to Seattle we had a stop in Las Vegas of about 45 minutes. We decided to deplane and stretch our legs. Much to our surprise the terminal was full of slot machines. I exchanged two one dollar bills for eight quarters. After playing six of my quarters I hit for six dollars. As this was my first time playing the slots, I decided to quit while I was ahead; I might add that my wife was also urging me to quit. When I went to the person who had exchanged my bills for quarters she informed me that I had to go to one of the cashiers to get bills for my quarters. Guess where the cashiers were located? They were on the other side of the terminal. I had to walk by many slots to get there, but I resisted the temptation to put in any more quarters. After I returned from getting my six dollars in paper money I decided to take a picture of Sally playing the slots. When we returned to Columbus I put this picture on the bulletin board at our church with the following notation: "Our church Financial Secretary in action. I wonder whose money she is playing with in Las Vegas." It received a lot of laughs, except from Sally.

When we arrived at the Embassy Suites, our hotel in Seattle, Carl, Gary, and some of the other Boosters were at the lounge having a drink. They gave us some bad news. Our star receiver, Joey Galloway, was suspended for the Washington game. This would have a devastating effect on our passing game. Buster Tillman replaced Galloway and although he was just as fast as Joey he didn't have the moves or experience that Galloway possessed.

While we were in Seattle we enjoyed seeing the sites. Ted's niece was a teacher at a high school in Tacoma. The school is named Stadium High School. It is located on the Bay and specializes in the arts. The school has a waiting list of potential students. In the past the building was owned by a railroad and has a large football stadium adjacent to it. It is state of the art, with artificial turf, where NFL teams like San Francisco have played exhibition games. One night she took us out to dinner and we enjoyed the best salmon I have ever eaten, fresh out of Puget Sound.

On the day of the game we had lunch on a boat that took us to the game. Many of the Huskies' fans travel to the games by boat and dock just outside the stadium. The game was a real bummer. The Buckeyes really missed Galloway and we trailed at the half 22 to 0. The Bucks made a game of it in the second half as they scored 16 points, but Washington tacked on a field goal and went on to win 25 to 16. Our tight end D.J. Jones dropped two crucial passes and the Bucks' defense was unable to stop running back Napoleon Kaufman as he racked up close to 300 all purpose yards.

Going into the Michigan game the Bucks were ranked number 22 and the Wolverines were number 19. At long last Cooper finally recorded a win over the hated Blue, his first of only two as head coach, in a convincing 22 to 6 win. The Bucks accepted a bid to the Citrus Bowl in Orlando, Florida, and their opponent was Alabama, a team they had never defeated. The number sixth ranked Crimson Tide were too much for the number 13th ranked Bucks as they lost another game to an SEC team.

The next bowl game I attended was the 1998 Sugar Bowl in New Orleans and the opponent was Florida State. After the disappointing loss to Michigan where we won the battle of the statistics but lost the game, the Buckeye fans had hopes that the Bucks would end the season with a win. If they did it would be OSU's first win over the Seminoles. In 1981 and 1982, they defeated the Scarlet and Gray decisively in back-to-back games in the Horseshoe.

When we checked into our hotel in New Orleans, my friend Ted and I were waiting at the elevator when I noticed a couple also waiting for the elevator. I whispered to Ted, "I think that's Bobby Bowden - the Florida

State coach." Just then he walked over and extended his hand and said, "Hi Buckeyes, my name is Bobby Bowden and this is my wife." Just then our wives showed up and we introduced them. Coach Bowden was very friendly and wished us well, except for the game. He went on to say that he told his friend John Cooper that he shouldn't take the Ohio State head coaching job. "I told him, John, you are a southerner, and you don't want to go up north and coach." The next day I was on the elevator going down to the lobby when the elevator stopped and Coach Bowden and two large young men got on the elevator. I was surprised when Bowden recognized me and said, "Hi, Larry I want you to meet two of my players" and he proceeded to introduce me to them. One of them was defensive end Andre Wadsworth, who was in the Buckeye backfield most of the game.

We had a good time in New Orleans but of all of the bowl games this site has very little in the way of attractions. Unless you are into drinking and expensive restaurants there isn't much to do there. Bourbon Street is quite an experience. Porn shops, transvestites and street entertainers, hustlers and con men are pretty much the main inhabitants of this famous street. As we walked down the street we were approached by Dave Maetzold, Sports Anchor for TV 4 in Columbus, and his cameraman. He asked me what I thought of New Orleans and I replied, "It's obvious that they don't have a vice squad here."

One of the things we did enjoy was a trolley ride that we took through the area where Tulane University is located. It was a very scenic ride. We also visited a beautiful white church and were thoroughly entertained across the street one day by two break dancers. Another highlight, at least for our taste buds, was our frequent visits to the Café Du Monde where we thoroughly enjoyed their Beignets. A Beignet is a soft roll covered with white sugar powder that is absolutely delicious with a hot cup of java. We also tried their famous jambalaya but we did not try the crawfish. They looked too much like what we call up north "craw dads" and they are used as bait for fishing.

The day of the game we attended the Buckeye Bash. The Buckeye band and the players and coaches had the fans really stirred up for the game. However, I winced at some of Coach Cooper's comments. He said "I wouldn't trade my quarterback for theirs, I wouldn't trade my running back for theirs, and I wouldn't trade my linebackers for theirs." And on and on he went. I thought to myself, I hope this doesn't end up being bulletin board material for the Seminoles .

As we entered the Superdome that night, I was impressed with the hugeness of it. I was very disappointed with some of our fans as they booed the Florida State marching band when they entered the field. This is not what you do, I thought to myself. It's bad enough to boo the football team, but not the band. The only team I ever boo is the Michigan Wolverines, but even then I don't boo their band.

I won't dwell on the game only to say that for the third time that OSU played FSU, they literally kicked the Buckeyes' butts again. The Bucks had no answer for the speed of their defensive ends as they either sacked or hurried both Germaine and Jackson all night.

The next day as we were checking out of the hotel we saw many of the Florida State fans as they, along with the team, stayed at the same hotel. I apologized to several of them about the behavior of some of our fans, especially the ones who booed their band. They thanked me and said the only other time that has happened to them was when they play Florida in the "Swamp." They also informed us that Coach Bowden did share Coach Cooper's comments that he had made at the Buckeye Bash. It really fired up the team and they were out to make Cooper eat his words. Well, they did and then some as they whipped the Bucks 34 to 17.

That was it for me as far as bowl games. I was retired now and on a fixed income and I did not intend to spend any more money on bowl games until OSU got a coach who could win them.

Chapter 15

Early Memories and Earle's Demise

Among my early memories of Ohio State football was going to watch practices in the spring and fall. The practice facility was located just south of the open end of the stadium. They had a chain link fence surrounding it but you could watch practice most of the time. There was one exception, the week of the Michigan game. They had tarps over the fences and nobody was allowed inside without the coach's permission. This was prior to the arrival of Woody Hayes. The practices weren't as open during the Hayes era. I remember watching practices under Carroll Widdoes and Wes Fesler and Woody in his early years before they built the Ernie Biggs facility.

I remember one game in the late fifties but I don't recall who the Bucks were playing that day in the Horseshoe. The starting quarterback was Jerry Fields and he was struggling in the first half and during the half-time fans noticed something going on at the practice facility south of the stadium. Woody had the center and quarterback practicing snaps. When the second half began Tom Matte was playing quarterback. It was Matte that Woody had taking snaps from the center during half-time. That was vintage Woody.

Before the Woody Hayes Center was built in the late eighties, the Ernie Biggs facility was a definite improvement over the previous practice area south of the stadium. However, it was a far cry from the multi-million dollar present day facility. When the Bucks moved into the new facility in 1987, Coach Bruce had the Quarterback Club meet there instead of the Fawcett Center, the usual meeting place. It was the week of the Iowa game and the Bucks had just lost two close games to Michigan State and Wisconsin. Earle gave us a tour of the new facility which would be later named the Woody Hayes Center as he had passed away earlier that year.

Earle's office wasn't quite ready, but he said if Woody could see it he would say, "Earle, you're getting soft." Woody's office at the Biggs facility was very austere which was fine with Woody. It was reported to consist of an inexpensive Steelcase desk and a stenographer's chair on rollers. Rumor has it that coaches or players would come in early in the morning and find him asleep with the projector still running and film all over the floor.

It's too bad Earle never got full use of the new office as he was fired that next week after the Bucks lost their third straight game. Iowa won on the last play of the game by a score of 29 to 27 as the Buckeye defense missed three tackles. Iowa's tight end Marv Cook scored from 23 yards out with 6 seconds remaining in the game. The next day's *Columbus Dispatch* had a picture of a very dejected Earle Bruce leaving the game with his hands in his pockets and his head down. I think he knew his days of being head coach of his beloved Buckeyes were numbered. It is nice that Jim Tressel has given both Earle and John Cooper offices in the Woody Hayes facility. It is just what you would expect from "Coach Vest."

It has always bothered me that some of the media and others act as if there wasn't any OSU and U of M rivalry until the ten years that Woody and Bo coached. This is ridiculous. It has always been an intense rivalry and only lost some of its luster when the Bucks went 2-10-1 under Cooper. Michigan players began making statements that this was not their most important game. Their most important game was against Michigan State or even Notre Dame. Now that Tressel has won 9 of 10 of their games I don't hear that comment anymore. I have been following OSU football since 1944 and it has always been the big game for both sides. I don't go back that far, but Head Coach Francis Schmidt defeated Michigan four years in a row in the late thirties and they were all shutouts. Then he lost to Michigan three years in a row and he was gone. The great Paul Brown lost two out of three to the Blue. His successor Carroll Widdoes won one and lost one in his short tenure as head coach. It was all downhill after that until Woody arrived. Even though Woody had a winning record versus Michigan, in the end he lost three in a row to the Wolverines and that, more than his slugging of the Clemson player, led to his dismissal.

Chapter 16

How I feel about that "Team Up North"!

Speaking for myself, beating "that team up north" is still what makes my season. I bleed scarlet and gray and would not be caught dead in anything even faintly resembling maize and blue. When I took my son to the Michigan game in Ann Arbor in 1975 we did not get anything to eat until we crossed the border into Ohio on our way home. He was in college at the time and had not eaten breakfast when I picked him up that morning. He asked if we were going to get something to eat at the game and I told him no, not in Michigan. I was even more determined not to buy any food when it was obvious they had increased the prices at the concession stands that day. When we crossed over into Ohio that evening we went to Wendy's in Sylvania, Ohio.

In 1976 my wife and I and our daughter travelled to South Bend, Indiana, to attend a wedding in Sacred Heart Church on the Notre Dame campus. My former manager John Chobanian's son Michael was getting married. It was a beautiful wedding and John and his wife Mary showed us around the campus. We saw the building where the "Gipper" had passed away. The popular version of that Notre Dame legend is that George Gipp told Coach Knute Rockne to tell the boys to win one for the Gipper. Rockne used that in his locker room speech and it motivated the Irish team. That is the Hollywood version but rumor has it that was not what happened. It seems George Gipp liked to bet on the ponies and what he told Rockne was to place a bet for the Gipper.

On the return trip to Columbus I noticed my gas gauge was getting close to E. We were on the Indiana turnpike and when I got off at the next exit there was a sign that indicated it was 1 mile to Sturgis and 3 miles to Howe. I headed north to Sturgis as I didn't think I could make it to Howe. About a hundred yards up the road there was a sign that said "Welcome to Michigan." I did a U-turn and just barely made it to Howe. There was no way that I was going to buy anything in "that state up north."

Chapter 17

Sales, Management, Radio, and Freelance Sports Writing

As I stated earlier, I was employed as a draftsman from 1955 until 1961 when I asked to be transferred from engineering to the sales department at Kinnear. Nothing like this had ever happened before and there was a bit of a struggle between the two departments, but I was granted the transfer. After five years I resigned and went to work for the Charles Bruning Company. They manufactured blueprint machines and various other products used by engineers, draftsmen, and architects. It was a good fit for me with my experience in drafting and sales. For the next 30 years I was employed by Bruning, first as a salesman and then as branch manager, regional manager, and district manager.

In addition to working full time in sales I also worked in radio at WHOK, a station in Lancaster, Ohio. I was a weekend all night disc-jockey for two plus years and then a Sunday morning newsman for two years. My shift was from midnight until eight am on Fridays and Saturdays. I really looked forward to the time period from seven to eight on Sunday mornings which was a simulcast on AM and FM. At that time I could play any of the music that was located in the studio. During the other hours I had to play what was referred to as Country and Western. WHOK FM 95.5 theme was "Sounds Country and Western." It was the only station in the Central Ohio area that played Country and Western music 24 hours a day. WHOK FM had a powerful signal which enabled them to reach into the Columbus area. In addition to being on the air I also did some part-time selling in the Reynoldsburg and Pataskala area. This was not my favorite type of music, but I didn't let that show when I was on the air. I was free to play any songs from the studio library plus any requests that came in from the listeners. Some of the artists that

I played at that time were Johnny Cash, Buck Owens, Willie Nelson, Sonny James, Connie Smith, Skeeter Davis, Loretta Lynn, and Stonewall Jackson. There was a rather new country artist that I liked by the name of Glen Campbell. He went on to be very popular in the late sixties and seventies with songs that were crossover hits. (A crossover hit is when an artist's music sells in two different formats. In this case Country and Pop music.) He also had a hit TV show on CBS in the late sixties. Johnny Cash also had a TV show for awhile and I found it interesting that someone had coached him on his diction for television. When I played some of his songs prior to his TV career his pronunciations were quite different . For instance, when he sang "The Ring of Fire" on his early records it was Ring of Far, and "The Orange Blossom Special" came out as Orange Blossom Spayshel. After appearing on TV, the new prints of his records were with the TV pronunciations. As I stated before, country music was not my favorite type of music but there were some others that I did enjoy hearing. Eddy Arnold, Marty Robbins, Jim Reeves, and Patsy Cline are some who come to mind.

I had some incidents that happened in my short radio career that I found amusing, although at the time I didn't. WHOK was a weather station for the area and there was a place located out behind the station where you could read the present temperature and a gauge for rainfall and snowfall. I would give the temperature on the air every 15 minutes. I would update it every hour by going out to the weather station to get the readings. I always selected a record that was of some length to permit me to get out there and back. One of my favorites was "The Ballad of Ira Hayes" by Johnny Cash. It was over seven minutes in length whereas most records are only two to three minutes long. I had two incidents relating to my weather duties. The first one was when I went out the back door and the door shut and locked me out. As an all night disc-jockey there wasn't anyone else there who could let me in so I had to break the glass in the door with my flashlight in order to get back in. I wrote a note to the station manager about how the glass got broken and they docked me $1.00 for the glass in my next paycheck.

My other situation happened on a very cold and snowy night. Just outside the back door there was a pipe that stuck up out of the ground about 18 inches. The snow had drifted up to the door and covered the pipe. When I went hurrying out to get the weather information I hit my shin on that pipe. When I returned to the studio and was reading the weather information I could feel the blood running down my leg and into my sock. I wanted to scream in pain but I couldn't while I was on the air.

One night my mind really played tricks on me. We often would get a phone call from the police informing us that there had been an escape from the Fairfield School for Boys. This was located a short distance from the station and this institution was for minors who had committed serious crimes. About 3 am I received a call that two boys had escaped and that they were dangerous and I should be sure the doors were locked at the station. This was no problem as I always kept the doors locked. About an hour or so later I was reading the meters in the studio, which was a requirement of the FCC. When I was returning to the console to play some more music I thought I saw someone at the front door. It startled me for a second or two and I thought it must be the escapees and one of them has on a sweater just like mine. Then it dawned on me that I was seeing my own reflection in the window of the studio where I was located. In retrospect I realized that when you're tired you can hallucinate.

One of my duties in addition to reading the meters in the studio and logging them in to the station FCC log book, was to turn on the AM transmitter at 4 am on Sunday mornings. At that time we would begin simulcasting. I did this every Sunday morning without an incident with one exception. One Sunday, when I turned on the transmitter sparks flew and the transmitter needles dropped. I had to call Charlie, the station engineer, and get him out of bed. I was not looking forward to this but there was nothing I could do. Charlie told me that it sounded like one or more of the fuses had blown. He instructed me to go into the back room where the new fuses were located. He went on to say that I needed to get the fiber covered pliers to use to install the new fuses. He stated that I needed to use those pliers in case I inadvertently touched something else in the transmitter which could electrocute me. I was one nervous guy trying to get those fuses changed with my hand shaking. All I could think about was the newspaper headline: Young Disc-Jockey found electrocuted in Country and Western radio station! I successfully changed the fuses and got back on the air without any dead air.

In the two years that I worked what is referred to as "the graveyard shift," I only fell asleep one time. From 4 am until 6 am on Sunday mornings I would play religious tapes like The Baptist Hour, The Christian Brotherhood Hour, etc. Most of the tapes were half an hour in length with one or two only 15 minutes long. I was playing this tape (I don't recall which one) that started at 5 and ended at 5:30. The next tape was to run from 5:30 until 6 am and then I would give the news at that time. Evidently I fell asleep sometime during the five o'clock tape. The next thing I knew I woke up and believe me nothing is as quiet as a sound proof radio studio. I suddenly realized that I had fallen asleep. I looked up at the clock on the wall and it read 5:40 am. There had been 10 minutes of dead air. I quickly started the next tape and then I realized I would have to stop it before it was time for the six o'clock news. As I recall it, the preacher was going strong when the hands on the clock were nearing 6 am. Normally the preacher would end his sermon and the choir would sing the closing hymn and at that time I would fade out the choir, give the station ID and play the jingle for the six o'clock news. Instead of doing this I had to wait for the preacher to take a breath and then fade out and hit the news jingle. After the news was over and I started playing records, I waited for the phone to ring off the hook with people wanting to know what happened to the sermon. There were no phone calls. Either there wasn't anyone listening to the station or there wasn't anyone listening to the preacher. I hope it was the latter.

During my time as a Sunday morning newsman I didn't have as many incidents happen to me as I did when I was working the graveyard shift spinning the platters. There were a couple that I would like to share with you.

My newscasts consisted of local, state, and national news. One morning during my newscast I read an item from the county engineer's office. It had stated that a certain county road beginning that coming week would have a two-ton load limit. When I got off the air and was in the newsroom compiling material for the next newscast, the phone rang. The caller asked to speak to Larry and I told him he was speaking to Larry. He said, "Larry, I would sure like to see that toad you were just speaking about during your newscast." I replied, "What toad?" He said, "You just said that the county road would have a two-ton toad limit starting this week." We both had a good laugh. I was glad that my boss wasn't listening that morning.

When I did the news it was in the adjoining studio to the control room where the disc-jockey was located. He would play the news jingle and then switch the mic on in the studio where I was located. That studio was also used for the taping of the Baltimore Apostolic Church program. This church was from nearby Baltimore, Ohio. There were a large amount of metal folding chairs stacked against the wall for their use during the taping. That sets the scene for what happened to me one morning. I would be in the newsroom preparing for my newscasts and would usually run into the studio just as the news jingle was playing. That morning when I opened the door to the studio I was shocked to find every one of those folding chairs set up and blocking my path to the table. When the disc-jockey turned on the microphone all the listeners could hear was me moving those chairs out of the way so I could get to the table and the mic. That was the first trick they pulled on the rookie newscaster. Later on they got me again. While I was reading the news I felt something cold and wet touch me. Somebody had let a large German Shepherd dog into the studio and I gave the rest of the news reading and petting the dog at the same time hoping to keep him from barking on the air.

In 1991 and 1992 I was a freelance sports writer for This Week, a weekly newspaper for various Central Ohio neighborhoods. One of my assignments was to interview Roger Harper, a defensive back for the Ohio State Buckeyes and former player for Independence High School in Columbus, and Marlon Kerner, another defensive back for the Bucks and former player for Brookhaven High School in Columbus. I was scheduled to interview them before practice at the Woody Hayes Center. While I was waiting for them I spotted Kirk Herbstreit in the hallway. I approached him and introduced myself and we began chatting about football. I will cover this conversation and more about Herbstreit in the next chapter.

Chapter 18

Kirk Herbstreit

This was 1991 and Herbstreit was the backup quarterback to Kent Graham. During our conversation I shared a story with Kirk about something that happened at a Quarterback Club meeting in 1989. At that meeting I asked Coach John Cooper the following: "When you were hired as the new head coach one of the first calls you made was to Kirk Herbstreit, the quarterback from Centerville High School who had committed to play for the Bucks when Earle Bruce was the head coach. It was rumored that Kirk was considering changing his mind and going to his second choice, the Michigan Wolverines. You wanted to make sure he was still going to be a Buckeye. Isn't that right?" Cooper replied, "Yes, that's correct." I then asked him, "What's happened to him and why is he not playing?" His reply was, "Well, we've been trying to talk him into playing safety, but he wants to play quarterback. Herbie is an option quarterback and we don't coach option football here." At that time Jim Colletto was the offensive coordinator and his offense was more suited for the pro style drop back passing quarterback.

This was true in Colletto's first three years at OSU, but in 1991 he took the head coaching job at Purdue and Cooper hired Elliot Uzelac as the new offensive coordinator. He coached option football. At the time, remembering Cooper's words at the Quarterback Club, I thought Herbstreit would get his chance to be the Buckeye signal caller. However, the new quarterback chosen to lead the Buckeyes in 1991 was Kent Graham. Graham had transferred from Notre Dame and sat out the previous year. His reason for leaving Notre Dame was because they were running option football. He wanted to be in a system that ran a pro style offense like Ohio State did under Colletto. So instead of using Herbstreit , a quarterback comfortable and experienced in option football, they named Graham the quarterback and he was now running the system that was the reason for his transfer from Notre Dame. Why not Herbstreit instead of Graham? When I asked Kirk about it, his reply to me was, "You sound like my mom." The next season, in his senior year, Herbstreit got his chance and led the Buckeyes to an 8-3-1 season and second place in the Big Ten. That one tie was with Michigan which Gordon Gee called the greatest victory in Ohio State history. No President Gee, a tie is like kissing your sister. I guess after four straight losses to the "Hated Blue" a tie looks pretty good. Especially when Gee renewed Cooper's contract for another four years just hours before Michigan humiliated the Bucks 31 to 3 in Ann Arbor the previous year.

After the 1992 regular season ended, the Buckeyes received an invitation to play in the Citrus Bowl in Orlando, Florida, on New Year's Day. Their opponent would be the Georgia Bulldogs featuring All-American running back Garrison Hearst. Leading up to that game Cooper made the following comment about his starting quarterback, "If the players had their way Herbie (Herbstreit) would have always been the starting quarterback. He lived on campus with the players whereas Graham was married and lived off campus." DUH!

Throughout Kirk Herbstreit's career at Ohio State I was one of his biggest fans, but since those days his behavior towards the Buckeyes has changed my feelings toward him. He seems to come across as more a fan of the Wolverines than the Buckeyes. I realize that now that ESPN signs his checks he must go along with their dislike of the Buckeyes. His comment after Terrelle Pryor signed to play for the Buckeyes really upset me as well as many of the Buckeye faithful. Before his career took off at ESPN he was a sideline reporter for WBNS, the radio outlet for Ohio State Football and Basketball games. He also had a daily sports call in show on that station. One time I called him and we discussed whether to root for Michigan or root against them. His view was to root for the Maize and Blue except when they played the Scarlet and Gray. I disagreed. In my opinion a true Buckeye fan never, ever cheers for "that team up north." I sometimes wonder if Herbstreit doesn't wish that he had gone to Michigan.

To end on a more positive note, I believe that Kirk Herbstreit is without a doubt the best college football analyst on television. Maybe his teaming up with Brent Musburger has also influenced his comments about Ohio State. Musburger has always come across as anti-Ohio State. I remember back in 1985 he was broadcasting the Iowa and Michigan game from Iowa City. The coaches were Bo Schembechler for Michigan and Hayden Fry for Iowa. Musburger never masked his love for Hayden. After Iowa upset Michigan that day he exclaimed, "Hayden Fry is the only coach, other than Woody Hayes, to win two in a row over Bo." I immediately wrote a letter to him informing him that his statement was wrong. Earle Bruce, the head coach for the Buckeyes defeated Bo and the Wolverines in 1981 and 1982. About a month later I received a hand written note on CBS stationary stating that I was right and he wished the Buckeyes success in the future. Six months later I received the exact same note from him. I guess he forgot that he already sent it. However, I never heard him correct his statement on television.

Chapter 19

Troy Smith

Speaking of quarterbacks, I believe that Troy Smith is the best to play that position for the Buckeyes. In addition to holding the record for most touchdown passes (30) in a season he is also the only pure quarterback to win the Heisman Trophy for the Buckeyes. Les Horvath, the first Heisman winner, played both quarterback and halfback and Vic Janowicz, the second winner, operated out of the single wing formation and was a tailback. In the single wing the quarterback and fullback were mainly blocking backs and the wingback was mostly a receiver and in some instances a runner and/or blocker. The tailback had the option to run or pass the ball. The modern day shotgun formation is similar to the single wing, and Troy would have been an excellent tailback in that formation with his ability to run and pass. Troy is also the only modern day quarterback to defeat Michigan three years in a row and owns three sets of gold pants. (Pryor has three, but against inferior opponents!) The only other quarterback that has that record against the hated Blue is Tippy Dye. He was at the helm when Francis Schmidt's Buckeyes defeated Michigan in 1934, 35 and 36.

Schmidt surprised the players at the banquet at the conclusion of the 1934 season when he presented the players with the first set of gold pants. Cornelius Greene has three sets of gold pants, but he was the backup quarterback to Greg Hare in the 1972 season. Greene earned his pants as the starting quarterback in 1974 and 1975. All of the great quarterbacks that have donned the scarlet and gray down through the years have not accomplished any of these feats. Not Kern, Schlichter, Tomczak, Hoying, Germaine, or Krenzel. I will grant you that Kern and Krenzel were at the controls when the Buckeyes won National Championships and Troy fell short in his one try in 2006. If Kern and

Krenzel had the kind of blocking from the offensive line that Troy had (5 sacks), I doubt if they could have led the Buckeyes to a national crown either. In addition to being the only quarterback at Ohio State to win the Heisman, Troy is also the only Big Ten quarterback to win the Heisman. That list includes some great quarterbacks such as Len Dawson, Bob Griese, Mike Phipps, Drew Brees, Chuck Long, to name just a few. In addition to winning the Heisman, Troy also won the Walter Camp Award, which is given to the Player of the Year, and the Davey O'Brien Award, which is given to the best Quarterback of the Year, in 2006. He was also named Player of the Year in 2006 by Sporting News. Troy was named Big Ten Offensive Player of the year in 2006. He took home the Silver Trophy as the Big Ten's Most Valuable Player in 2006. Only three other Buckeye quarterbacks won that trophy, Cornelius Greene in 1975, Art Schlichter in 1981, and Joe Germaine in 1998. In 2006 he was named Big Ten Offensive Player of the Week five times. Troy had over 1000 yards of total offense as he threw seven touchdown passes and rushed for one in three wins over the hated Blue. Troy is the only OSU quarterback to throw 4 touchdown passes in a Michigan game which he accomplished in 2006. Troy threw for 408 yards against Notre Dame in the 2006 Fiesta Bowl which is second only to Art Schlichter's 412 against Florida State in 1981. Troy's career record at Ohio State as a starter was 25 – 3 for a .893 average which is second only to Rex Kern's 28-2 and a .933 average. In 2006 Jim Tressel stated, "I think Troy Smith is the best player in college football."

However, everything was not always positive in Troy's OSU career. In 2004 he accepted $500 from a booster and the result was his suspension from the Alamo Bowl and the first game of the 2005 season. That proved to be very costly for the Buckeyes 2005 season in which they lost two games that they should have won. Justin Zwick was the starting quarterback for those games and he led the Buckeyes to a win over Oklahoma State in the Alamo Bowl and Miami (Ohio) in the season opener. Zwick and Smith shared quarterback duties in the Texas game. Zwick threw a perfect pass in the end zone to tight end Ryan Hamby, which could have put the game out of reach for Vince Young and the Longhorns. However, Hamby bobbled and then dropped the pass. Young later led the Longhorns to a 25 to 22 win. Two weeks later a rusty Troy Smith threw an interception that was returned for a touchdown in the

Penn State game and later fumbled the ball while leading the Bucks to a possible winning drive late in the game. Defensive end Tambia Hall blew by Ryan Hamby and blind-sided Troy which caused the fumble.

It has always been my opinion that 2005 was the year that the Bucks could have won the National Championship. Defense wins championships. The 2005 squad with A.J. Hawk, Bobby Carpenter, and Anthony Schlegel as linebackers, with Quinn Pitcock on the line and Ashton Youboty and Donte Whitner in the secondary was a championship team. They would have been a difficult team to defeat. Unfortunately because of that $500 it cost the Bucks a chance to prove it. The 2006 defense was not as good, as Florida proved convincingly.

Chapter 20

Les, Vic, Hop, Archie, Eddie, & Troy and Missing Two Traditions

In evaluating the OSU Heisman winners I believe that you have to put them in two different categories. Les Horvath, Vic Janowicz, and Howard Cassady played both offense and defense during their careers at Ohio State. All three were defensive backs. Archie Griffin, Eddie George, and Troy Smith were strictly offensive players. All three have established Buckeye records. George has the rushing records for a game and a season. Troy, as mentioned before, has the record for most touchdown passes in a season and Archie has the record for career rushing yards, as well as the NCAA record for the most 100 yd. games in a career.

Hop Cassady was just as outstanding on defense. His 88 yard interception return for a touchdown in the 1954 Wisconsin game was a key play in the Bucks 1954 undefeated season which led to a National Championship.

The Heisman winner with the most talent is without a doubt Vic Janowicz. Vic ran, passed, kicked off, kicked extra points, punted and played excellent defense. His performance in the 1950 Iowa game (83-21) was truly unbelievable. He scored two touchdowns, passed for four more and kicked ten extra points and he played very little in the second half. In the "Snow Bowl" game of 1950 he kicked a 38-yard field goal into the teeth of a swirling wind, blowing snow and from a difficult angle.

Archie Griffin will always be remembered for his outstanding achievement of winning the Heisman Trophy two times. Archie on or off the field is truly a class act.

There are two yearly events from the past that I miss. The first is the Senior Tackle which was always held the week of the Michigan game. If the Bucks were at home it was on Friday nights and if they were playing in Ann Arbor it was on Thursday nights. I started attending Senior Tackle when Woody was the head coach and continued under Earle Bruce. I've never understood why Cooper discontinued this tradition as part of the hype for the game with the hated Blue. I think he scrapped the Tackle to try to play down all of the pressure building up to a game he just couldn't figure out how to win.

The second event was the team picture day the first week of practice in August. After the media was finished, the fans were invited onto the field at the "Shoe" to meet the players, take pictures, and get autographs. I looked forward to this every year and I have some excellent pictures of players and coaches during the Bruce and Cooper years. When Jim Tressel arrived they held this in the stadium concourse. Players were seated at tables to sign autographs and in later years they did this on the field. It got to be a zoo, and finally Tressel ended it. I believe the reason was that it was impossible to sign all of those autographs in a restricted time frame. Many of the autograph seekers were dealers and others who sell the autographed items. They spoiled it for those fans that just wanted to greet and meet the players, take pictures and get autographs, and had no ulterior motives of profit.

Chapter 21

Seating Controversies

In 1986, a fan wrote a letter to *Dispatch* Sports Editor George Strode complaining about the way Ohio State had narrowed the seating space in the Horseshoe. Strode replied that he had checked with Mike Dolan, superintendent of OSU athletic facilities, and the Ohio Stadium seats were made a uniform 18 inches wide in 1973 when Fiberglas covering was installed. The seats were painted and numbered again that summer but the 18 inch uniformity was maintained. The next week I wrote to Strode and came to the defense of the fan who complained about the width of the seats. I went on to tell him that my seats in section 22C row 20 seats 19 and 20 are not a uniform 18 inches. I measured them at 14 inches, and seats 21 and 22 were only 9 inches. I offered to meet Mike Dolan at 22C with a tape measure at his convenience. The following week he replied to my letter with the following statement: Mike Dolan tells me you are correct about inconsistencies in the widths of 22C in the stadium. Dolan apologized to those who had 9 inch and 14 inch wide seats in 22C. Dolan said some seats in 22C were as wide as 24 inches, the result of carelessness in repainting and renumbering of the seats in the summer. "The Bucks are on the road the next two weeks and we are going to reapportion the seats correctly to 18 inches each before the next home game." At that next home game with the Minnesota Gophers the game was much more enjoyable as everyone in 22C had more room to watch the Bucks shut out the Gophers 33 to 0. The couple sitting next to us in seats 21 and 22 asked me if I had written a letter to the *Dispatch* Sports Editor about our narrow seats. I replied that I had and he and his wife thanked me profusely.

Speaking of seats, I had another unpleasant situation when Ohio State opened the Schottenstein Center in 1998. I was informed that seat locations in the new basketball facility would be based on priority points. I had purchased season tickets since 1976 and I was assigned 162 points. I realized that unless I purchased seat licenses I would not be located in the lower bowl, although I thought this was unfair to the loyal fans that had supported the team during the lean years of walk-ons as well as the good years. Being retired, my fixed income would not permit me to purchase seat licenses, however I believed that I would have decent seats in the Terrace Level. Imagine my surprise when a friend of mine with only 5 points ended up with better seats than I was given. After my letters and phone calls to Richelle Simonson, Ticket Director, were ignored, out of desperation I wrote to Andy Geiger, the Athletic Director. He responded immediately and agreed that something was wrong and he would speak to Simonson about this. I did not hear from her. I attended the Basketball Appreciation Banquet a short time later and I approached Ms. Simonson. She remembered my letters and phone calls but said that I must be mistaken about my friend having better seats than me. I suggested that she look it up on her computer and I was sure she would see that I was right. I then reached into my breast pocket of my suit and pulled out my letter from Mr. Geiger. Her eyes widened and she said to call her on Monday at her office after 9 am. To make a long story short I was moved down from row 13 to row one, seats one and two. The next year I was moved to seat 11 and 12, further from mid-court. Meanwhile my friend's were moved down from row three to row one and one section closer to mid-court. I gave up. No more phone calls or letters.

I have been a loyal fan of the basketball Buckeyes since the days of Robin Freeman and the games in the State Fairgrounds Coliseum. I've had season tickets since 1976 and I really miss St. John Arena. It was a much more intimate place and could really get loud and intimidating for OSU opponents. The Schott is just too cavernous and many of those in the seat license seats do not cheer and make noise. To them it appears to be more of a social occasion rather than a sporting event. I feel that Ohio State let down their true loyal fans when they moved to the Schottenstein Center. We, who supported the team when they were only putting six or seven thousand fans in the seats during the Randy Ayers' walk-on days, have not been treated fairly for our loyalty. If you can't pony up the big bucks for seat licenses you are relegated to the balcony.

Chapter 22

I Miss the OSU Men's Basketball Boosters Club!

I guess it's the sign of the times, but another activity I miss as a longtime supporter of the OSU Men's basketball program is the booster club. Although the supporters of the women's basketball team still have their booster club, the demise of the men's began with the hiring of Jim O'Brien. Although I was never a member of Fred Taylor's Rebounders Club, I was a member of Eldon Miller's Center Circle Club, and Gary Williams and Randy Ayers Fast Breakers Club. The Center Circle members met at the old Arlington Arms motel on Dublin Road for a lunch buffet during the basketball season. For $10 we had a nice buffet and after lunch Coach Miller would discuss the previous game and the upcoming opponent. Eldon was a bit testy at times, especially if you asked him about playing zone defense. We were given a ticket with a number on it when we entered the meeting and later a number would be drawn and that person won the privilege of sitting on the bench at the next home game. In January of 1982 my number was drawn and I got the thrill of sitting on the bench at the Purdue game. I entered St. John Arena at the door for the press where I was greeted by assistant coach Gerry Sears. He escorted me to the locker room where I met all of the players, coaches, managers and trainer. The starting five were Clark Kellogg, Tony Campbell, Granville Waiters, Larry Huggins, and Carter Scott. It was exciting and interesting to listen to Coach Miller talk to the players during time outs and overhear him discuss strategy with his coaches. After warm ups we went back to the locker room and then returned in time for the national anthem and introductions of the starters. It was a hard fought game and unfortunately the Bucks lost in overtime 66 to 60. I was warned before the game not to say anything to the officials that could result in a technical being called on the bench. I had to remind myself that I was not a fan sitting in my seat and could not express my displeasure at some of the officials' calls. I was able to control myself but Mike Bordner, the trainer, was not and he caused a technical to be called on the bench. When it was called, Miller turned and stared at me, but Bordner admitted he was the guilty one. I didn't linger in the locker room after the game as there was sadness, frustration, disappointment, and some tears in the room. I thanked Coach Miller for the experience and headed for the parking lot. It was a great experience that I will always treasure. I only wish the ending had been better.

When Gary Williams arrived in 1986, the opportunity to sit on the bench was discontinued and he retained the booster club, he just changed the name to the Fastbreaker's Club. We began meeting at the OSU golf course dining room and although Williams was known to turn the air blue during games, he was careful how he spoke at the meetings, especially if any women were present. I remember one time I took my wife to one of the meetings and during his talk, he said damn and hell a couple times, and when he spotted my wife in the audience he apologized for his language. Gary was a dynamic coach and Buckeye fans were sad when after only three years of exciting basketball Williams decided to accept the head coaching job at his alma mater Maryland. His short stint as head of the Buckeye cagers included two 20-win seasons and one 19-win season with a win over Kentucky in the NCAA tournament in his first year. The best he could achieve in the Big Ten was two .500 seasons. On the minus side he never defeated arch rival Indiana in three tries and he lost two out of three to in-state rival Dayton. On the plus side, he successfully recruited Jim Jackson who would go on to be an All-Big Ten and All-American player for the Bucks under Williams successor, assistant coach Randy Ayers.

Randy in his first three years won two Big Ten titles -- one co-championship and one outright title. Some of Randy's critics complained that he did it with Williams' players and anybody could win with players like Jackson, Brown, Jent, and Carter. However, as I would point out to those naysayers, if it wasn't coaching but strictly talent, why did Michigan coach Steve Fisher fail to win any titles with the "Fab Five"? Three of those five, Rose, Howard, and Webber, were high NBA draft selections and only Jim Jackson was a high draft pick by the NBA. Unfortunately Randy made some poor recruiting choices in the ensuing years which resulted in problems to the program. Near the end of his time as the head coach, his team lacked great talent and as a result it was difficult to win many games. Shortly after he fell on the ice and broke his ankle I told him, "Randy, if you didn't have bad luck, you wouldn't have any luck at all." I really liked Randy both as a person and as a coach.

Randy continued to meet with the Fastbreaker's Club and he added another feature that was really nice. Once a season he had a pizza party at St. John Arena. We could bring kids, age 15 and under, and they could eat all the pizza they wanted at no charge and the adults only had to pay $5 for their pizza and soft drinks. We would watch practice and after practice the kids could go down on the floor and shoot hoops with the players. The coaches and players would sign autographs and pose for pictures. It was a great time for all concerned. I took several of my neighborhood kids and my pastor's son and they had a ball.

When Jim O'Brien arrived as head coach he ended the Fastbreaker's Club luncheon and we only had one pizza party and that was held next door at the French Field House. We were not permitted to attend practice and the kids were not allowed on the floor. The following spring I ran into the guy who was in charge of the basketball luncheons and he said O'Brien wouldn't do those type of things for less than $1000 a plate. I guess you can take the guy out of the east coast, but you can't take the east coast out of the guy.

Chapter 23

I'm an OSU round ball fan too.

Although I am mainly an OSU football fan, I also have enjoyed the Buckeye round ball games for many years. I started following the Buckeyes when they played their games in the Fairgrounds Coliseum where Robin Freeman set a lot of OSU records. Also on some of the teams of the fifties were Paul Ebert and Frank Howard. Of course the most memorable team was the 1960 National Champion Buckeyes with Lucas, Havlicek, Nowell, Roberts, Siegfried, and the sixth man Dick Furry. Today the team is often referred to as the Lucas, Havlicek, and Knight team. Originally the team was referred to as the Lucas, Havlicek, Seigried, and Nowell team, but as Bobby Knight became more famous as a head coach at Indiana, they started adding his name with Lucas and Havlicek. This is so wrong, as Knight was strictly a sub and was never a starter in his years at Ohio State. Jerry Lucas was the best rebounder I ever saw. He is first, second, and third in most rebounds and also holds the top three spots in rebounding average. One time I was attending a Center Circle luncheon and sitting at my table was Frank Truitt, who was an assistant coach when Lucas played at OSU. I asked him what made Lucas such an outstanding rebounder and he replied, "Jerry just had that instinct to know when to go up for a rebound. Many times his opponents were on their way down when he went up to get the rebound. They just jumped too soon and Jerry always went up at the right time He also seemed to have that sixth sense and know where the ball would come down." I remember hearing about Lucas when he was playing for Middletown and he was being recruited by all of the big basketball programs. The game I remember the most was one that I'm sure he would choose to forget. It was the last game of his senior year at Middletown. The Middies were riding a 76-game winning streak and Lucas had never tasted defeat in his entire high school career. Their opponent in the semi-final game of the State High School Tournament was the North High Polar Bears coached by Frank Truitt. North upset Middletown that night 63 to 62 and they were the toast of Columbus town. However, they lost the championship game to Cleveland East Tech when Jim Stone hit a shot from mid court at the buzzer sending the game into overtime. In the first overtime neither team scored and according to the rules at that time, which later were changed, the second overtime was sudden death. East Tech scored first and the game was over for the Cinderella team as they lost a disappointing game 50 to 48. It was rather ironic that the coach of the team that gave Lucas his first high school loss would eventually be one of his coaches during his illustrious career at Ohio State.

I would be remiss if I didn't mention the great success of the Buckeye basketball team under Head Coach Thad Matta. In addition to three Big Ten titles and three Big Ten Tournament titles, he led the Bucks to the NCAA championship game and won the NIT title. In his six years he has posted 20 or more wins each season and a school record 35 wins in 2007. Who can ever forget the thrilling win over undefeated and top ranked Illinois in the regular-season finale when Matt Sylvester hit a three pointer with seconds remaining in the game?

The loss to Florida in the 2007 NCAA championship game was especially difficult as it came in the aftermath of the number one ranked Buckeye football team's loss to Florida earlier that same year. In retrospect I believe that Mike Conley would not have departed for the NBA after his freshman year if the Bucks had lost the NCAA tournament game to Xavier. At the time I was just as pleased as all Buckeye fans were when Ron Lewis hit the three pointer to send the game into overtime. However, if he had missed and the Buckeyes had been eliminated from the tournament, I believe that Conley would have returned for his sophomore season. Conley's stock rose as a result of his play in the rest of the tournament leading up to and including the title game. It was a no-brainer that Greg Oden would be one and done, but I don't believe that Coach Matta thought Conley and Daequan Cook would leave early. Conley's departure left a real hole at point guard during the next several years for the Buckeyes. Cook's departure was a real shocker as he did not impress as a Buckeye. Ron Lewis won the starting role over Cook during the season, which didn't set too well with Daequan or his mother.

The Buckeyes really struggled at point guard until Matta made the bold move to install Evan Turner at that position for the 2009-2010 season. Turner had earned the nickname of "Turnover Turner" in his previous seasons with the Buckeyes. However, in his new role Turner not only became a good point guard, he finished the season winning Player of the Year in the Big Ten and national honors as well. His number will surely hang from the rafters at Value City Arena in the future as one of the best ever to don the scarlet and gray for the Buckeyes. His shot to win the Michigan game in the Big Ten Tournament will be a Buckeye Classic someday. My nephew Larry Mitchell and I watched the game on television at the Smokey Bones restaurant in Reynoldsburg, Ohio. The restaurant was deadly silent when Michigan took the lead with just seconds to play. When Turner hit that three point shot as time expired, the restaurant erupted in one big cheer. It is something that I will always treasure among my memories of OSU basketball. It was especially gratifying to watch the Maize and Blue clad fans go from a premature celebration to a look of shock and disbelief.

It would have been great if Turner had decided to return for his senior year, but I believe he made the right decision in choosing to go to the NBA. The only goal he hadn't achieved was winning the National Championship. There's certainly no guarantee that if he had chosen to return that the Bucks would have won the title. With their incoming freshman class and Turner returning they would be a pre-season favorite to win it all. However, they still could have fallen short of the NCAA Championship. If you don't believe that, just ask Kentucky, Syracuse, and Kansas.

Chapter 24

Recent Painful Losses

Getting back to football and our most recent painful losses, I would like to express my thoughts on those games. The loss to USC in September 2008 in Los Angeles on nationwide television was another embarrassment for the Buckeyes. There is no second guessing that game, the Bucks just got their butts kicked. However, their other two losses that season could have been victories. The first one was the loss to Penn State which was decided on a crucial fumble by freshman quarterback, Terrelle Pryor. Prior to his fumble, Chris "Beanie" Wells ran for what appeared to be a first down, however the official gave the Bucks a terrible spot and it resulted in a third and less than yard. With a more accurate spot the play by Pryor would not have occurred. The other game was the heartbreaking loss to Texas in the Fiesta Bowl. If Anderson Russell had tackled the receiver instead of trying for the interception there would not have been enough time for Texas to score. Another play that was costly was Dan "Boom" Herron scoring with too much time remaining. The Buckeye coaching staff should have called two running plays by Maurice Wells and they would not have scored a touchdown and used up precious time on the clock. They could have kicked a field goal and Texas would not have had sufficient time to move down the field and score.

In 2009 the rematch with USC replays showed that the USC player did not cross the goal line for their first touchdown after Pryor's pass was picked off.

In the Purdue debacle where Pryor's four turnovers were very costly, the Bucks could have won that game despite those errors by Pryor. When the game was close in the first half, Kurt Coleman stripped the ball and recovered the fumble near the five yard line; however, the official said the play was blown dead. No one heard a whistle blowing the play dead. This was crucial because Purdue came into the game having turned the ball over frequently. This could have changed the momentum of the game as the Purdue players could have thoughts of "here we go again." Another turnover that played a part in the outcome of this game was Ray Small's fumble of a punt inside the 10 yard line. In spite of Pryor's miscues, the Bucks could have won the game. The bottom line is the loss should not have been placed on one player, Terrelle Pryor.

In the remaining games of the 2009 season Pryor began to live up to his recruiting hype, especially his performance in the Rose Bowl. He headed into his junior season being one of the candidates for the Heisman Trophy and the chance to tie Troy Smith's record of being the only OSU quarterback to win three pair of gold pants with a win over Michigan. Of course the devastating loss to Wisconsin, the only blemish on the Bucks 2010 season, has to be one of my all-time painful losses.

Chapter 25

2010-2011

I delayed finishing this book until after the 2010 football season and the 2010 -2011 basketball season. The pre-season polls had the Buckeye football team ranked in the top five and Terrelle Pryor as one of the favorites for the Heisman Trophy. The scuttlebutt was that the Buckeye basketball team would be ranked in the top ten in the nation. This was based on the fact that Head Coach Thad Matta had the best freshman class since the Thad Five in 2006-2007. With David Lighty, Jon Diebler, William Buford, and Dallas Lauderdale returning, the Bucks would have the experience to go along with the talented youth. The question mark was who would play the point guard position? The loss of Player of the Year Evan Turner would be a negative. The previous season there was much skepticism about playing Turner at point guard. That turned out to be a good move, but can Matta repeat that success this season?

Getting back to the football team I knew the Bucks had three difficult games on their schedule, the Miami Hurricanes, Wisconsin, and Iowa. The Hurricanes and their fans would be chomping at the bit to avenge Miami's defeat in the National Championship game in 2003. Many of the Hurricane fans still feel that official Terry Porter robbed them of a victory in Tempe when he called pass interference with a late flag. I would have been more worried about this game if it were played in Miami as it will be in 2011. The other two games that would be a challenge are both road games. Playing at Camp Randall Stadium is always a difficult game. To add fuel to the fire it was, thanks to television, a night game. I vividly remember the night game in Madison in 2003 and how ugly the fans were as the Badgers upset the Bucks, ending their 19 game winning streak. The 2008 game was a real nail biter until freshman quarterback Pryor led the Bucks to a come from behind victory.

After convincing wins over Marshall, No. 12 Miami, Ohio U. and Eastern Michigan, the Bucks just squeaked by Illinois in this first road game of the season. After a home win over Indiana and due to the upset of number one Alabama, the Bucks headed to Madison ranked number one in the nation. After a slow start the Bucks trailed 21 to 3 and although they battled back it was too little too late and they suffered their first and only defeat of the season. This loss knocked them out of any chance for the National Championship. They went on to win their sixth straight Big Ten Championship as they shared the title with Wisconsin and Michigan State.

The Bucks were invited to play Arkansas in the BCS Sugar Bowl. With the exception of the loss to Wisconsin and Pryor not being in the running for the Heisman, it was another successful Buckeye season. Adding icing to the cake was the Bucks eighth straight win over their arch rival Michigan. Tressel has now won 9 out of 10 games with the "Team up North."

On December 23rd disaster struck the football program as five players were suspended for selling their Buckeye memorabilia to a tattoo parlor. Terrelle Pryor, Daniel Herron, Devier Posey, Mike Adams, and Solomon Thomas would have to sit out the first five games of the 2011 season. However, the NCAA ruled that they could play in the Sugar Bowl. This decision did not sit well with the media or the fans. Coach Tressel did obtain a commitment from the guilty players that they would return for their senior year instead of going to the NFL. This made it a little more tolerable, although I thought all five should have been benched for the Bowl game. Ironically one of the tattoo lovers, Thomas, made a key interception that sealed the victory over the Razorbacks. Pryor was voted the MVP of the game which I thought should have gone to Cameron Heyward who was a monster on defense.

What bothers me the most about this whole fiasco is that these five players thought so little of their Big Ten Championship rings and the gold pants they earned by beating Michigan, that they would sell them for tattoos. As I stated earlier in this book, Pryor has the opportunity to be the first and only Ohio State quarterback to defeat Michigan four times and have four sets of gold pants. As much as I always want to defeat that "Team up North" it upsets me that he who cares so little for the symbol of winning this game would have this honor. My hope is that by the time they play Michigan that Pryor is not the starting quarterback.

When it was later revealed that Coach Tressel knew about this incident as far back as April 2010, I was shocked. I have always admired Tressel not only for his coaching ability but for his character, especially his integrity. I have read his books and in one he states "It is easier to tell the truth than to explain a lie."

Although the football Buckeyes fell short of their goal of winning the National Championship and the tattoo scandal and suspensions has cast them in a bad light, the basketball team helped ease some of the pain. Thad Matta's team was picked to finish third in the Big Ten, but surprised all of the so-called experts, by winning both the regular season and tournament Big Ten championships. They finished the regular season 29 and 2. They were the consensus number one team in the nation and received the top number one seed in the NCAA tournament. However, once again they were knocked out of the tournament in the Sweet Sixteen round. Last year it was Tennessee who defeated the Bucks, as Player of the Year Evan Turner missed an off balance shot as time expired. I always thought that Turner should have passed the ball to a wide open Jon Diebler on the wing. Diebler had an off night from outside of the arc, but I thought he had a good look and he was overdue. Diebler was the guest speaker at our church's men's meeting in August 2009 and I asked him if he thought he could have made that shot if given the chance. He replied, "The ball was in the right person's hands at that time." I guess when you consider the way Turner had performed all year Jon was right. But, I still think the Bucks would have won the game if Diebler had been given the ball at that point in time. With that win the Bucks could advance to the Elite Eight and possibly the Final Four. I guess I could add this to my lists of If's that I covered about the Buckeye football teams in chapter 13 of this book.

This time it was Kentucky that eliminated the Buckeyes in the Sweet Sixteen when Brandon Knight made a short jumper in the last seconds of the game. William Buford had a good look from outside the arc but it was off target and instead of being the hero with the winning shot, he finished the night 2 of 16 on field goal attempts. I told my wife before the game, "If Buford has a hot hand tonight the Bucks will win easily, but if he doesn't the Bucks will be in trouble." In retrospect I wonder if Matta had called time out and set up a play the outcome might have been different. I really believe that if the Bucks would have defeated the Wildcats they would have gone all the way. If they could have pulled that game out on a night when they shot 32.8% they would have had their bad game out of their system. Here I go again If only, If only ...

As the old saying goes, "It's an ill wind that blows no good."! After the game Sullinger and Buford announced they would return next season. Many of us thought that Sullinger would join Oden, Koufos, and Mullens and be one and done. Prior to the season beginning there was also speculation that freshman Deshaun Thomas would be one and done too. He also announced he would return the next year.

So what does 2011 look like for the Buckeye football team? Much will depend on whether or not the NCAA adds additional penalties on Coach Tressel. If they come down hard on him he may be forced to resign. Ohio State is not going to act until the NCAA rules. Athletic Director Gene Smith and OSU President Gordon Gee have stated that Tressel is their coach regardless. However, I'm sure they remember how they got burned when they fired OSU basketball coach Jim O'Brien before the NCAA ruled and it cost the university millions of dollars when O'Brien sued them and won his suit.

Needless to say I wrote this chapter prior to May 30, 2011. I was shocked to hear that Coach Tressel had resigned. An upcoming article in *Sports Illustrated*, indicating possible additional NCAA violations by the football program, was the apparent reason for Tressel resignation. Luke Fickell, the interim head coach for the first five games, was named the head coach for the entire 2011 season. I'm sure this news brought shouts of joy from the fans of other Big Ten schools, especially in Ann Arbor, Michigan. In my opinion the first thing that Fickell should do as head coach is to tell those five tattoo lovers they are no longer welcome as members of the Buckeye football team. There is bound to be resentment among the players towards these five as their actions led to Tressel leaving.

When the news broke later that Terrelle Pryor was forgoing his senior year at Ohio State and entering the NFL supplemental draft, I was overjoyed; one down and four to go. As I stated earlier, I did not want to see Pryor be the only OSU quarterback to defeat the hated Blue and receive four sets of gold pants.

Even though I'm extremely disappointed in Tressel's behavior in all of this, I still think he is a good coach and should have been retained. The Bucks should be able to win their first two games with Akron and

Toledo, but could have difficulty winning their first road game in Miami with an inexperienced quarterback and head coach. The next two games at home with Colorado and Michigan State could further test the Buckeyes. If they win the game with the Hurricanes they should defeat the Buffaloes. The real test will come against a very good Spartan team. They have many returning lettermen from their Big Ten Co-Championship team of 2010. However, which team will show up the one who soundly defeated Wisconsin or the team who looked bad in their loss to Iowa and their humiliating loss in their bowl game to Alabama?

If the Bucks can be 5 and 0 when the suspended players return they could still salvage the season. That of course is a big if. There are several questions about this 2011 version of Buckeyes. If the replacements for Posey, Herron, Adams, and Thomas performed well, do you bench them in favor of the tattoo lovers? Will the Bucks be able to replace the seven starters they lost from the 2010 highly rated defense? How will all of this affect the morale of the team? Looking down the road will it hinder the Bucks recruiting? Only time will tell. 2011 promises to be an intriguing season.

Even though the Bucks will have to replace David Lighty, Jon Diebler and Dallas Lauderdale, they still will be loaded with talent if not experience in the 2011-2012 season. These are some of the questions facing Thad Matta as he approaches his 8th season as the head coach of the Buckeye cagers. Will freshmen Amir Williams and Shannon Scott be able to crack the starting lineup? If Williams can play the post that will free up Sullinger to play the power forward, however will Jared be able to rebound as well from this position? Can Deshaun Thomas live up to his hype coming in last year, that he was a possible one and done player? Can Sullinger improve his jump shot away from the basket? Which lineup will work best: Buford, Craft, incoming freshman guard Scott, Thomas and Sullinger or Buford, Craft, Scott, Sullinger, and Williams? It looks like the Bucks will have the most depth they've had since the 2006-07 season. Will Matta be able to keep all of these blue chip recruits happy or will some transfer out due to lack of playing time?

2011-2012 looks to be an interesting season for both the Buckeye football and basketball programs.

hapter 26

My Favorites

GAMES BY THE DECADE

I only had one favorite game in the forties and that was in November 1944. As I stated earlier in this book my first time in the Horseshoe was as a Cub Scout. The Bucks played the Pittsburgh Panthers. Although the stars of that team were All-Americans Les Horvath, Bill Willis, Jack Dugger and William Hackett, the player that I admired was running back Ollie Cline. He became my favorite Buckeye and the next year he was named an All-American.

My favorite games in the fifties were the 1954 and 1955 Michigan games and the 1957 and 1958 Iowa games. The 1954 Michigan game was most memorable for the Bucks great goal line stand. The Wolverines had the ball first and goal at the four yard line late in the third quarter with the score tied at 7 to 7. On fourth and inches the Bucks stopped Michigan and on Michigan radio the announcer Bob Ufer screamed that Michigan scored but the official ruled it Ohio State's ball on the six inch line. Making that stop was Jim Parker, Jim Reichenbach, Francis Machinsky and Hubert Bobo. That was in days of one platoon football and those four also played on offense. Parker and Reichenbach were guards, "Moose" Machinsky was a tackle and Bobo was a linebacker and fullback. After that great goal line stand, the Buckeyes marched 99 2/3 yards to go up 14 to 7. Contributing to that drive were two big runs, one by Jack Gibbs and the other by Hop Cassady. Later in the game Cassady scored another TD to make the final score 21 to 7. That win evened the series at two wins each since Woody became the OSU head coach. Woody went on to many great wins in his 26 years as the head coach, but that 1954 win had to be one of his biggest. The Bucks went on to defeat Southern California in the Rose Bowl to finish their season undefeated with a 10 and 0 record and were crowned the National Champions for the first time under Woody. The 1955 win was especially sweet as it was Ohio State's first win in Ann Arbor since 1937 when

Francis Schmidt's Buckeyes shut out the Wolverines 21 to 0. The best the Bucks could do at the Big House was a 20 to 20 tie in Paul Brown's first year as head coach in 1941, and a 7 to 7 tie in 1949 under head coach Wes Fesler. What I remember most about that game is the way Ohio State dominated the Blue on defense. They permitted Michigan to cross the 50 yard line only one time and that was via a penalty. To pour salt in the Wolverine wounds, the Buckeye victory sent Michigan State to the Rose Bowl. In those days there was a no repeat rule in going to the Rose Bowl. Ohio State had gone the previous year which made the second place team in the Big Ten the representative in the Rose Bowl. If Michigan had won they would have represented the Big Ten. Instead their much hated in-state rival went. Near the end of the game as it became apparent what this loss meant, some of the Michigan players lost their composure and their All-American end Ron Kramer was ejected from the game. There were lots of chants, "unpack your bags you're not going anywhere," as the Bucks prevailed 17 to 0.

Two of the other games in the fifties that are among my favorites were against the Iowa Hawkeyes in 1957 and 1958. I attended the game in Ohio Stadium in 1957. The winner of the game would be the Big Ten Champion and be headed to the Rose Bowl. Iowa had a flashy offense featuring quarterback Randy Duncan. It turned out to be a low scoring defensive battle and Iowa had the lead 13 to 10 late in the fourth quarter. The Buckeyes were less than 70 yards from pay dirt with the Big Ten title and trip to the Rose Bowl hanging in the balance. What happened next was an amazing performance by the offensive line and the powerful running of fullback Bob White. White carried the ball on all but one play and capped off the drive with a powerful five yard run for the go ahead touchdown. Forest Evashevski, the Iowa head coach and former Michigan running back, said after the game, "We knew what was happening, but we were powerless to stop it." It was vintage Woody Hayes, three yards and a cloud of dust football as the Bucks just lined up and ran it right down the Hawkeyes' throat. I and the people seated around me kept saying, surely they are not going to keep running off tackle, but they did and it worked. Woody was not going to change the play until Iowa showed they could stop it.

The 1958 game was not televised and Iowa had already clinched the Big Ten title and trip to Pasadena and were a 14 point favorite in the game played before a sold out Iowa stadium. The Hawkeyes went on to defeat Oregon State in the Rose Bowl and ended up second in the final

AP poll. However, on November 15 in Iowa City, Ohio State handed the Hawkeyes their only loss of the season 38 to 28. It was all offense and the score was tied four times before the Bucks scored ten unanswered points in the fourth quarter. I watched the game with my son at St. John Arena on closed circuit television. They had four screens hanging in the center of the arena and the crowd was large and loud. Fullback Bob White and halfback Don Clark led the ground attack and scored all five of the touchdowns. Dave Kilgore added a field goal near the end of the game. The Bucks played without starting quarterback Frank Kremblas and his backup Jerry Fields did an excellent job of running the offense. Of course, all he had to do was hand the ball to White or Clark. It was one of the most exciting games I have ever watched, with White running up the middle for big gains and Clark going wide. The blocking of the offensive line was a thing of beauty led by Dick Schafrath and Jim Houston who went on to star with the Cleveland Browns.

I have three favorite games of the sixties and two are games with Michigan. The first one is the 1961 game in Ann Arbor and it is one of my favorite games for several reasons. First it was the most points ever scored on the Wolverines by the Buckeyes in a 50 to 20 victory. (It was later equaled in a 50 to 14 win in 1968.) It was a spectacular show of offense led by quarterback Joe Sparma, halfbacks Bob Klein and Paul Warfield with All-American fullback Bob Ferguson. It was especially sweet to score that many points at the Big House. It was later revealed that the reason the Buckeyes offense wasn't its usual conservative style, was because one of the assistant coaches was calling the plays from the press box. That assistant was Bo Schembechler, who later would be calling the plays for those hated men of Blue.

With the score 48 to 20 Woody elected to go for two and it was successful. When asked why he went for two instead of one with the game all but over he said he wanted the final scores to add up to 70 in honor of long-time assistant coach Ernie Godfrey's 70th birthday. Later there were two other reasons given for going for two. One was that Woody said, "I went for two because I couldn't go for three!" Another reason given was it was a payback for Fritz Crisler, head coach for Michigan, going for two in the Wolverine butt-kicking of OSU 58 to 6 in 1946 on our turf. Although Woody wasn't the coach back then, he knew his history of the rivalry. The 1961 win was the second in a row over the Maize and Blue and Woody went on to win in 1962 and 1963. Those wins gave him the distinct honor of being only the second coach to defeat "that team up north" four straight. The other coach was Francis Schmidt who not only defeated the Wolverines four in a row, but also shut them out in those very sweet victories. Woody and Schmidt would have been proud of Jim Tressel and his amazing feat of seven straight over the hated Blue.

The other Michigan game was the 1968 win in Ohio Stadium. It was a close game as the Bucks only led 21 to 14 in the third quarter. The Michigan fans were small in numbers, but loud and confident with many of them seated in my section of the horseshoe. Suddenly the Bucks, led by fullback Jim Otis, broke the game open when they scored 29 unanswered points in the last two quarters. The defense rose up and shut the Wolverines down with three interceptions and several tackles for losses. I remember rejoicing while the Michigan faithful quietly exited the stands.

The other game in the sixties happened that same year in the third game of the Super Sophs' season. It was the opening game of the conference schedule and the Bucks were hosting the Purdue Boilermakers, the previous season's Big Ten champion. A quirk in the schedule had the Boilermakers returning to Ohio Stadium after humiliating the Bucks 41 to 6 in the Horseshoe the previous season. Purdue was ranked No. 1 in the nation and featured quarterback Mike Phipps and a very talented running back in Leroy Keyes. Although the Buckeyes had won their first two non-conference games with Southern Methodist and Oregon easily, no one knew if the Bucks were up to this test. It was scoreless at the half which spoke well of the Buckeye defense as Purdue had been averaging 41 points in their first three wins. Jack Tatum established himself as a star on defense as he held Keyes to an all-time low in yardage. Phipps was sacked numerous times and OSU cornerback Ted Provost intercepted a Phipps pass and returned it for a touchdown to give the Scarlet and Gray the lead. Later in the game Bill Long replaced an injured Rex Kern at quarterback and on his first play he went back to pass, and finding no one open, scrambled for a touchdown. The final score was only 13 to 0 which wasn't a true indication of how the Bucks whipped the Boilermakers as they held a large advantage in statistics. Although the 1968 team is renowned in Buckeye football lore as the team of "Super Sophs," it was two seniors who had key plays in the win over Purdue. Cornerback Ted Provost and quarterback Bill Long who scored the two touchdowns were both seniors. Without them the Bucks may have started the 1968 conference at 0 and 1. In 2008 much was made of Jim Tressel's decision to replace senior Todd Boeckman with freshman Terrelle Pryor and comparisons were made to Woody's decision to replace senior Rod Gerald with freshman Art Schlichter at quarterback in 1978. However, no one mentioned Woody's decision in 1968 to start sophomore Rex Kern over returning senior quarterback Bill Long. At least in the Schlichter case, Gerald was still on the field although at slot-end, not as a quarterback. In Long's case he was relegated to the bench and as the season progressed lost his job as Kern's backup to another sophomore, Ron Maciejowski.

The 1969 Rose Bowl is one of my favorites because it was the Bucks' first undisputed National Championship since the 1954 team who also defeated the Trojans to win the title. The game itself was exciting and when Southern Cal went up 10 to 0 it didn't look good for the Buckeyes, but they came back to tie the score before the end of the first half. The final score was 27 to 16 but the Trojans final TD was controversial. It appeared that Buckeye defensive back Mike Polaski had intercepted a pass in the end zone with less than a minute to play, however the official ruled it a USC touchdown. It was either an interception or an incompletion. There was no way it was a touchdown. It didn't matter as the Buckeyes won, but the final score should have been 27 to 10. Everyone who had 7 in a football pool must have been ticked off.

The 1970 Michigan game in Ohio Stadium will always be one of my favorites because the Bucks avenged their upset loss to the Wolverines the previous season. I also remember Woody saying after the game that "We beat them at their own game." What he was referring to was a play that Michigan used against the Buckeyes in their 24 to 12 upset the previous year in Ann Arbor. It was a two tight end formation with a delay-type play by the halfback. Woody borrowed it from Michigan and Leo Hayden ran it to perfection as he gained over 100 yards. How sweet it was and although I didn't see the game in person I enjoyed every minute of it on television.

The 1974 and 1975 games I saw in person and they are two of my all-time favorites. The 1974 game was a favorite because the Bucks won without scoring a touchdown, sealing the come from behind win with four field goals. Tom Klaban, a walk-on soccer style kicker, was the hero of that game and Mike Lantry, the Michigan kicker, was the goat as he missed a crucial field goal with seconds left in the game. His miss denied the Maize and Blue the league title and trip to the Rose Bowl. It was the third straight Ohio State-Michigan game in which he missed very makeable field goals costing the Wolverines dearly. I loved it!

The 1975 game was especially pleasing as I was in the end zone with most of the Michigan student body in Ann Arbor and had received much abuse during the game as I described in great detail earlier in this book. It was one of the greatest comeback victories in my many years of following this intense rivalry. The stars of that game were many on both offense and defense. Two key interceptions would be the difference between victory and defeat. After tying the game at 14, Ray Griffin's interception and return set up Pete Johnson's touchdown to put the Bucks up 21 to 14. Craig Cassady's interception of freshman quarterback Rick Leach's pass sealed the victory for the men of Scarlet and Gray.

In 1977, the Oklahoma Sooners came to Columbus for their first ever meeting with the Buckeyes. The Sooners totally dominated the game at the beginning and led 20 to 0 at the end of the first quarter. The Sooner defense had completely shut down the Buckeye offense and it didn't look good for the Scarlet and Gray. I was seated near some very rowdy Oklahoma fans and they had these red and white paddles that said "Go Sooners!" on them. They kept waving them in our faces and gloating over the score. Suddenly in the second and third quarters the Bucks offense came alive and they scored 28 unanswered points. Speedy quarterback Rod Gerald and the running of Ron Springs and freshman fullback Joel Payton and a couple turnovers created by the Buck defense turned the game in OSU's favor.

The Buckeyes were driving late in the fourth quarter when Greg Castignola, who was now playing quarterback for the injured Gerald, fumbled at the Oklahoma 43 yard line. The Sooners began to move the ball like they had earlier in the game. The Buckeye defense rose up and stopped the Sooners at the Buckeye 12 yard line on a fourth and four run by Elvis Peacock. However, the Buckeyes nose guard Aaron Brown was called for being offside and the Sooners had new life. Peacock then scored from the one yard line with less than two minutes to play. Trailing 28 to 26 the Sooners tried a two point conversion to tie the score. They tried an option pitch but the Buckeye defense stopped them short of the goal line to preserve the two point lead.

Everyone in the stadium knew with a little over a minute to play the Sooners would be trying an on-side kick. Woody put his good hands players on the field to better his odds of recovering the on-side kick. The ball travelled the required ten yards, took one bounce and ricocheted off third string quarterback Mike Strahine's chest and Oklahoma recovered. The Sooners moved the ball to just short of the twenty and with three seconds remaining in the game they sent their kicker, Uwe von Schamann on the field to try a field goal. Woody called time out to try to freeze the kicker. All of the OSU fans were on their feet screaming and making as much noise as possible and praying that he would miss the kick, but he didn't.

In retrospect when you look at that game you realize how many things had to happen for Oklahoma to grab that victory from the jaws of defeat. If Castignola hadn't fumbled the Bucks could have ran out the clock or got close enough for a field goal to put the game out of reach. If Aaron Brown had not jumped off side the Sooners would not have scored their last touchdown. If Mike Strahine had recovered the on-side kick and if Rod Gerald had not been injured he would have been playing quarterback and might have been in on the on-side kick attempt. But as Earle Bruce always said, "If ifs and buts were candy and nuts we would all have a Merry Christmas." Speaking of Earle Bruce, in 1983 he coached the Buckeyes to a great win over the Sooners in Norman to avenge the Bucks' 1977 loss. I will discuss that game when I talk about my favorite games of the 1980s.

The next year in which I have two favorite games is 1979. This was the first year with Earle Bruce as the OSU head coach. There was much doubt about this year and Bruce's ability to succeed a legend, in the person of Woody Hayes. Earle quickly silenced those doubters as he led the Buckeyes to an undefeated regular season and a trip to the Rose Bowl for the first time in four years. The turning point in that season came in the fourth game when the Buckeyes travelled to Los Angeles to play the UCLA Bruins. Trailing 13 to 10 late in the fourth quarter the Buckeyes scored the winning touchdown with less than a minute to play. Sophomore quarterback Art Schlichter completed a pass to the tight end Paul Campbell in the end zone on an option play from the three yard line.

This was one of many coaching decisions that Bruce made that year which contributed to the successful season. Many of Woody's fans were not giving Earle Bruce credit for this winning season. The comment often made was he was winning with Woody's players. They seemed to forget that the 1978 team finished 7-4-1 and had lost for the third year in a row to Michigan and in those losses failed to score a touchdown with Woody's players. When Earle assumed command of the Bucks he made some crucial decisions when it came to his lineups. He inserted Tim Burke, a third string tackle, at left tackle and he had a career year at that very crucial position. He started two other third stringers, Tim Sawicki and Jim Laughlin, at middle guard and outside linebacker respectively. Another key move was replacing Gary Dulin with Luther Henson at left defensive tackle. Probably the best move was when he switched Gary Williams from defensive back to slot-end and he along with junior Doug Donley gave the Buckeyes a potent passing offense. Getting back to the UCLA game, during the week of practice leading up to the game with the Bruins, the Bucks lost both of their tight ends to injury. Earle made the decision to convert second string fullback Paul Campbell to tight end and Campbell caught the pass that gave the Buckeyes their come from behind victory. One other memory from that game was the revelation a year or so later that the Bruin player who blocked the punt that led to UCLA's first touchdown had never attended a class while playing for the Bruins.

The other favorite game in the 1979 season was the come-from-behind win over Michigan in Ann Arbor. It not only was the Bucks first victory at the Big House since 1975, but it also marked the first time the Buckeyes scored a touchdown against "the Hated Blue" since that 1975 game. That came in the third quarter on a pass from Art Schlichter to tight end Chuck Hunter. The score that gave the Buckeyes the victory came on a blocked punt late in the game when Earle called for a 10-man rush. The punt was blocked by linebacker Jim Laughlin, a player who seldom saw the field under Woody. Ironically Art Schlichter never defeated Michigan in the Horseshoe, but picked up two sets of gold pants for his victories in 1979 and 1981 in Ann Arbor.

Speaking of that game in 1981, it tops my list of favorite games in the 1980s. This was my first trip to Ann Arbor with the Buckeye Boosters. The reason this game made my list of favorites came down to one game-turning play. Every Buckeye fan will recall "The Block!" Trailing 9 to 7 late in the game, quarterback Art Schlichter rolled right on a quarterback option play and as he started to cut back, fullback Vaughn Broadnax threw a block and proceeded to knock down three Maize and

Blue defenders and Schlichter walked into the end zone to seal the win. I remember how loud and long we celebrated after the game as the Michigan fans exited in silence. No one is as obnoxious as Wolverine fans when they win and no one is as quiet when they lose. I loved it!

My next favorite game of the 1980s happened in Norman, Oklahoma, in 1983. First I would like to give you a little background leading up to this game. The company I worked for, Bruning, had merged with a software house in Tulsa, Oklahoma, to add a CAD (computer-aided drafting) system to our product line. I was promoted to Regional Manager for the new CAD Division. I travelled to Tulsa for a week of training and sales and marketing strategies. Several of the employees of the software company were Oklahoma fans and they proceeded to brag about the Sooners and how they were going to kick the Buckeye's butts. They had a running back by the name of Marcus Dupree, who had an outstanding freshman season and was the pre-season favorite for the Heisman Trophy. The Buckeye defense shut him down and he departed with some type of injury early in the game. Even with a field temperature of 135 degrees the Buckeyes ran and passed their way to a very convincing 24 to 14 win on national television. Tight end John Frank had a huge day in receptions and it couldn't have happened to a more deserving guy. Leading up to the game there was some speculation whether Frank would play or not, as it was a Jewish holiday. During warm ups several of the Sooner fans were heard shouting to Frank on the sidelines, "Hey Jew boy, welcome to Oklahoma, are you afraid to play our Sooners?" Apparently this motivated Frank and although he was an outstanding player he seemed to be a notch better on that very hot and humid day in Norman. Oklahoma head coach Barry Switzer was looking for his 100th coaching victory, but he would have to wait another day for that number as the Bucks avenged their loss in 1977 in the Horseshoe. The next week at the Quarterback Club Earle Bruce told us that Dupree left the game because he got a little "boo-boo"! Bruce said that his problem was that he had never been hit as hard as the Buckeyes hit him and he didn't want to play anymore. After the Buckeye game his stock in the Heisman race went downhill. I made sure my friends in Tulsa put their money where their mouths were as I collected on some small wagers.

1984 was the year that Ohio State made a great comeback against Illinois in one of the most exciting games in the history of the grey edifice called "The Shoe." After a heartbreaking loss to Purdue to open the Big Ten season, the Bucks returned to Columbus to face the defending Big Ten Champion Illinois. The Illini along with Iowa and the Bucks were pre-season favorites to fight it out for the 1984 title. After a little over one quarter of play the Illini led the bewildered Bucks 24 to 0, and it looked like the rout was on. To some OSU fans it brought back memories of the 41 to 6 drubbing of the Bucks by the Purdue Boilermakers in Ohio Stadium in 1967. It was one of the worst beatings in the giant horseshoe in the coaching career of Woody Hayes. However, history would not repeat itself, as the Buckeyes came storming back scoring 21 unanswered points and only trailed 24 to 21 at the half. We Buckeye fans sat stunned as we just witnessed an offensive show by both teams. We didn't realize at the time when Ohio State was behind 24 to 0, that tailback Keith Byars had looked into the TV camera on the sidelines and said, "We are coming back!" He made good on that promise as he led the Bucks to a thrilling win when he scored a touchdown with just seconds remaining in the game as the Bucks won 45 to 38. Byars scored five touchdowns and ran for 274 yards breaking Archie Griffin's school record of 246 yards. His fourth touchdown of that game will be the one that Buckeye fans will remember the most. In that 67 yard run he lost his shoe at the Illinois 35 yard line and ran diagonally across the field with one shoe off as he crossed the Illinois goal line.

The next week at The Quarterback Club Earle Bruce told us that when the score was 24 to 0, he paused and looked up to the sky and said, "You are not going to let the bad guys win this game, are you?" Illinois head coach Mike White had a reputation for not always playing by the rules.

In selecting my favorite games in the 1980s I most certainly would have to pick the 1985 Iowa game in Columbus. The Hawkeyes were ranked number one in the nation and were undefeated coming into Columbus to play the eighth ranked Scarlet and Gray. Iowa had the top rated passer in the nation in All-American quarterback Chuck Long and an All-American running back Ronnie Harmon. The Bucks were leading the Big Ten in offense but were ranked ninth in pass defense. The morning of the game the local newspaper, The Citizen-Journal, ran an article stating that the woeful Ohio State secondary had little chance against the top passer in the nation. That would appear to be the only motivation the Buckeyes needed. They did get some additional motivation from 1984 Heisman Trophy runner up, Keith Byars. Byars had re-injured his foot and was unable to suit up for the game, but he gave an emotional pre-game speech, which along with the newspaper article, fired up the Bucks. Long was intercepted four times and was held well below his normal passing yardage. The Bucks prevailed 22 to 13 with 17 of their points coming as a result of Iowa turnovers. Woody watched the game from home where he was recovering from a heart attack. I'm sure this win brought back memories of one of his biggest wins over the Hawkeyes when they defeated Forest Evashevski's team in 1957 to win the Big Ten title. Although this win did not result in a conference title, it never-the-less was one of Earle Bruce's finest coaching jobs as he bested that wily old fox Hayden Fry. The week before the game I engaged in some friendly banter about this game with one of the men in our company's marketing department. He was an Iowa graduate and was very confident that the Hawkeyes would win this game. When I called him on the Monday following the game all he could talk about was the weather conditions for the game and how that favored the Buckeyes. There was a light rain throughout the game, but as I told him it was equal for both teams and his team was ranked number one and he had the number one quarterback. He had no reply.

The 1986 Cotton Bowl win over the Texas A&M Aggies was memorable for two reasons. First it was a super performance by the Buckeye defense that totally confused Aggie quarterback Kevin Murray. He threw a Cotton Bowl record five interceptions, two of which the Bucks ran back for touchdowns. Earle Bruce stunned the fans both in attendance that day and watching on television when he appeared on the sidelines in a business suit and fedora. It was his attempt to quiet some malcontents that had made comments about his unprofessional appearance. It was alright for Woody to wear a short sleeved shirt, tie and baseball cap, but Earle was criticized for being too casual. At last with this win Earle finished the season 10-3, hopefully putting to rest the nickname uttered by some of "9 and 3 Earle." It was after this season that Arizona came calling and offered Earle a five year contract at more money than Ohio State was paying him. There would be less pressure than the OSU job and the warm Arizona climate made it even more tempting. After his five year contract was up what better place to retire than Arizona. Athletic Director Rick Bay persuaded Earle to stay and Earle being such a Buckeye at heart turned down the Arizona offer. In hindsight it was a mistake as the very next year both Earle and Bay would be forced out at Ohio State. I always admired Rick Bay for refusing to fire Earle when that horses a—Jennings ordered him to do so. Assistant Athletic Director Jim Jones was named Athletic Director as he did Jennings dirty work for him. I always figured that Jones went to Jennings and said, "I'll do it, Ed.

I'll do it." And lo and behold he was rewarded for what he did. In my opinion he turned out to be "one of the worst ADs" in Ohio State history. As I have stated earlier in this book, I was never in favor of the firing of Earle Bruce, but I accepted it if the new coach could take the Bucks to a higher level. Well, he didn't and I will always wonder if Earle had won that 1980 Rose Bowl and the National Championship and if Woody had lived longer, would Earle have survived?

Of course the 1987 Michigan game has to be one of my favorites. It was Earle's last game as the head coach and with a win he would exit with a winning record against the "hated Blue." I was there and I was so glad to see Earle go out in style with a win over Bo and the scUMmies.

I approached 1988 with some skepticism as the John Cooper era began. In his first game as head coach Cooper's Buckeyes looked very impressive in a convincing victory over Syracuse. However, the next week they were totally humiliated 42 to 10 by Pittsburgh in Pitt Stadium. After two games I didn't know what to think of the Buckeyes and their new coach. After playing an almost flawless game against the Orangemen of Syracuse they were a fumbling, penalty prone mess against Pitt. One of my favorite games occurred the next week as the LSU Tigers visited Columbus. The previous year the two teams played to a 13 to 13 tie in Baton Rouge. That game had a controversial ending as I detailed earlier in this book. I didn't know which team was going to show up, the one who defeated Syracuse or the one that got their butts kicked by Pittsburgh. LSU led 33 to 20 with less than five minutes remaining in the game. The Buckeyes fought back and the Tigers led 33 to 29 with a little over a minute left in the contest. On third and seven at the LSU 20 the Bucks scored the winning touchdown and the crowd went wild as the Buckeyes had staged an amazing comeback over a stunned LSU team. However, the very next week the Bucks played poorly again and were soundly defeated by Illinois. There was more of the same throughout that season as the Bucks finished 4-6-1.

This would prove to be somewhat of a pattern for Cooper as he had several come-from-behind wins in his 13 years as head coach of the Buckeyes. One of those wins was the 1989 win at Minnesota. This game is one of my favorites of the 1980s. The Gophers jumped out to a 31 to 0 lead and the rout appeared to be on. The Bucks managed to score a touchdown with two seconds remaining in the first half. A successful two point conversion made the score 31 to 8 at half-time. With less than a minute to play in the game the quarterback, Greg Frey, completed a pass in the Gopher end zone to Jeff Graham for a heart-stopping 41 to 37 win. That win equaled the largest comeback win in NCAA history. It also may have saved John Cooper's job at that point in time. The other memorable comeback victories under Cooper were the 1990, 27 to 26 win over Iowa at Iowa City and of course one of his best games at Ohio State the 20 to 17 win over Arizona State in the 1997 Rose Bowl.

One of my favorite games of the 1990s was the victory over Penn State in Happy Valley in 1995. Being humiliated 63 to 14 the previous year made this win even sweeter. Due to a quirk in the schedule the Bucks had to play back-to-back games at State College. The Nittany Lions and their fans were extremely confident that they would once again trounce the visiting Buckeyes. My wife and I travelled to this game with the Buckeye Boosters and we just got to our seats in time for the kick-off. State College is not an easy place to get to and on several trips we have arrived there late and had to hurry to our seats. In more recent years the Boosters stay just off Route 80 north of State College instead of staying in Sharon, PA, as they did in the past.

The Lions jumped out to a 10 to 0 lead after one quarter and the Bucks then scored 14 in the second half to take a 14 to 10 lead at the half. Trailing 25 to 21 with a little over three minutes remaining in the game the Buckeyes mounted a drive which was kept alive by a great catch by tight end Rickey Dudley. Dudley was tightly covered by a Penn State linebacker but managed to catch a perfectly thrown ball by quarterback Bob Hoying for a 32 yard gain. With just under two minutes to play Eddie George took the ball into the Lions' end zone for the winning touchdown. George atoned for a first quarter fumble that led to a Penn State field goal and the 10 to 0 lead. Buckeye fans stayed in their seats celebrating the victory that avenged the devastating loss the previous year. The Lions fans sat there in disbelief as their Nittany Lions and their beloved Joe Pa were now 1 and 2 against the Buckeyes since joining the Big Ten. Today, since joining the Big Ten Joe Pa and his Lions are 6 and 12 versus Ohio State. Joe Pa's lifetime record is 8 and 14 versus the Buckeyes.

The two games that the Buckeyes played and won against Notre Dame in 1995 and 1996 have to be among my favorites of the 1990s. It had been 60 years since the first meeting between these football powerhouses and the excitement in Columbus was at an all-time high. With the exception of the Michigan games there was nothing to compare to the feelings in Columbus leading up to that last Saturday in September in 1995. The speed of receiver Terry Glenn and the powerful running of Eddie George was more than the Irish could handle. The Buckeyes avenged their loss in Ohio Stadium in 1935, the year I was born. They followed that up with a convincing win in South Bend in 1996 as they evened the series between the two schools. Although the margin of victory wasn't as great this time the Buckeyes' superiority was every bit as evident as the beating they administered the previous year. Instead of Eddie George and Terry Glenn this time it was Stanley Jackson and Pepe Pearson doing the damage. Unfortunately these two wins came too late for me for a special reason. One of my salesmen, who was a big Notre Dame fan, used to tease me by saying that Woody Hayes and Ohio State were afraid to play the Irish. He would say that Woody so feared Notre Dame that when he flew west he would make sure the pilot didn't fly over the Golden Dome. He took me to a Notre Dame game back in 1977. It was a cold rainy dreary day and the Irish were playing the Miami Hurricanes. This was prior to Miami becoming a major power on the national scene. The Irish won the game but at one point the outcome was in doubt and this was the scenario. Miami had the ball inside the five yard line and was threatening to score and take the lead. A woman seated next to me had her rosary out and was praying. It was unreal. However, it worked as Miami didn't score.

That was my first and only time to see a Notre Dame game in South Bend. It was quite an experience. At the souvenir stands in addition to selling badges, pennants, hats, etc. supporting the Irish, they also were selling badges and other items with the picture of the Pope on them. When the Irish marching band came out to perform I commented to my friend that their lines were kind of crooked. He replied, "We're not known for our band, but our football." My salesman Chris passed away in 1986 and never knew that the Bucks had scheduled two games with his beloved Irish. Maybe it is better that he didn't know as he surely would have been sadly disappointed by the results of those two games. I also took great pleasure in the two wins as the quarterback in both games for the Irish was the much heralded Ron Powlus. This is the guy who Beano Cook predicted would win not only two Heisman Trophies, but four. The Buckeye defense blitzed him and our defensive backs took his receivers out of the games.

The 1997 Rose Bowl is my last favorite game of the 1990s. I did not attend this game for the following reasons. I was there for the 1975, 1980, and 1985 Rose Bowls and the Bucks lost all three of them to USC. I didn't want to spend all of that money and see them lose again. The second reason was Coach John Cooper's bowl record which wasn't much better than his record against Michigan. Going into the Rose Bowl his bowl record was 1 and 6. I watched the game on television and when Jake "the snake" Plummer scored to give the Sun Devils the lead 17 to 14 with less than two minutes to play I almost turned the TV off. Much to my surprise the Bucks rallied to win with just seconds remaining. I couldn't believe my eyes. At last a Rose Bowl win for the first time since 1974. This was without a doubt John Cooper's finest hour as a head coach at The Ohio State University. His decision to put Joe Germaine in at quarterback was a stroke of genius on Coop's part. "Thank you John, maybe you have turned the corner" was my thought as we watched the Rose Bowl trophy presentation.

The 2001 Michigan game in Ann Arbor has to be one of my favorite games of the new century. Our new head coach Jim Tressel had indicated that we would be proud of our Buckeyes on this day many months before this game. We certainly were proud of those men in Scarlet and Gray as they upset the Wolverines. Michigan was ranked number 11 in the country coming into the game and was the favorite over the unranked 6 and 4 Buckeyes. The week before the Buckeyes had lost to number 12 Illinois when the Illini intercepted a Craig Krenzel pass and ran in for a touchdown to seal the victory. Prior to this game Krenzel was the third string quarterback for the Bucks. The starting quarterback Steve Bellisari had been benched when he was charged with a DUI. Second string quarterback Scott McMullen was named the starter for the Illinois game. I was serving on jury duty that week when we heard the news about Bellisari's arrest. Everyone in the jury room thought that the season was over. Although Bellisari was not a great quarterback, he must have been better than McMullen or he wouldn't be the starter. I along with many other Buckeye fans never understood Cooper's decision to play Bellisari at quarterback. Ohio State was the only school to recruit him as a quarterback. All the other schools were recruiting him as a safety. I believe that Bellisari could have been a possible All-American safety. Instead the Bucks had a potential All-American or at least an All-Big Ten safety playing quarterback.

When Tressel arrived I was hoping that he would not play Bellisari at quarterback. His reasoning was that he had the experience as he had been the quarterback for the two previous seasons. In the Illinois game McMullen was benched in the second half in favor of Krenzel. With Krenzel under center the Bucks made Tressel's prediction come true as they defeated the "hated Blue" 26 to 20. Krenzel led the Buckeyes to a 14 and 0 record in 2002 and the National Championship and many of the Buckeye fans, including yours truly, wondered what would have happened if Krenzel had been the quarterback sooner.

2002 was a terrific year with many memorable games. One that comes to mind was the encounter with Purdue in West Lafayette, Indiana. I attended that game with the Buckeye Boosters. Our seats were located in the south end zone bleachers in the lower section, not the best location for viewing the game. As it turned out it was a horrible location for the most important play in the game. With fourth down and one late in the game and the Bucks trailing 6 to 3, everyone thought Tressel would send in Mike Nugent for a tying field goal. Instead they went for it and not a run for the first down, but a pass in the end zone to take the lead. That successful completion from Krenzel to Michael Jenkins would be shown many times in the highlight reels of the 2002 undefeated season. Unfortunately I missed seeing it as my view was blocked by fans standing up in front of me. It's times like this that I wish I had stayed home and watched it on television. It was great to be there and be part of the celebration, but not to see one of the most crucial plays of that championship season was disheartening.

The next week I did stay home and watch the game as the Bucks visited Champaign-Urbana to face Illinois in back-to-back road games. This was the first of two overtime games the Bucks played in that championship season. In both cases there should not have been an overtime played. I explained my reason for the game with Miami earlier in this book. In the Illinois game television replays clearly showed that quarterback Craig Krenzel on a keeper had scored a touchdown. Instead the officials ruled that he was down just short of the goal line and the Bucks kicked a field goal. If the officials had made the correct call there would have been no overtime and the Bucks would have prevailed 23 to 16 which was the final score after an unnecessary overtime.

The 2002 Michigan game has to be one of my favorites of this year as it clinched the Big Ten title and the trip to the desert to play for the National Championship. It was a hard fought contest that came down to the last play of the game when Will Allen intercepted Michigan quarterback John Navarre's pass in the end zone. I remember two things about that game. First how much the first half reminded me of the 1996 game when the Buckeyes dominated the game but could only score three field goals. In this game it was Michigan that ran up 200 yards on the Bucks but only scored nine points via three field goals. In the 1996 heartbreaker the Wolverines scored 13 unanswered points in the second half to win 13 to 9. This time the Bucks prevailed 14 to 9 for their first win over "the Hated Blue" in the Horseshoe in three tries. The second memory is watching that last second pass from Navarre headed towards a wide open receiver in the end zone and feeling "oh no, here we go again another undefeated season ruined by those blankety-blank men in blue." Then what seemed like coming out of nowhere was Will Allen, snatching victory from the jaws of defeat. Freshman running back Maurice Clarett, nursing a sore shoulder, had a key pass reception to set up the winning touchdown. That touchdown was scored on a beautifully executed quarterback option with the other Maurice, Maurice Hall scoring. Hall also scored the winning touchdown the week before in overtime at Illinois. Hall had been overshadowed by Clarett that year but without his two touchdowns the Bucks would never have had the chance to play for the National Championship. The following May of 2003 Hall was the guest speaker at the men's meeting at my church and he not only spoke about football, but he also gave a Christian witness that was memorable. He may have lacked some of the talent of Clarett, but as a person he would prove to be head and shoulders above the controversial Clarett in the ensuing years.

The BCS National Championship game with Miami on January 1st 2003 has to be one of my favorite games if for no other reason than it was the Buckeyes first national title in 34 years. In addition to that it was also the best BCS National Championship game played at that point in time if not ever. It was especially sweet because no one gave the Bucks a chance against the talent and speed of the Hurricanes. The talking heads on ESPN were especially annoying as they predicted scores like 34 to 7 and 41 to 0. I think the thing that surprised all of the so-called experts, was how fast and good the Buckeye defense was that night. I gave my thoughts and opinions on this game earlier in this book. I'm looking forward to the game with the Hurricanes in 2010 in Columbus. Terrelle

Pryor will be a junior and it could be his last year wearing the scarlet and gray and I look for him and the Bucks to have a great game on national TV. At last maybe it will silence those Hurricane fans who thought the Bucks, with the help of the official, stole that 2003 game.

The 2004 Michigan game has a special place in my memories. It was the first home game with Michigan that I missed in 16 years. In October 2004, I had lung surgery and did not recover as quickly as doctors had predicted. Instead of a hospital stay of six days, I was there for 12 days. I seemed to be doing better after five days when my oxygen level suddenly dropped to 50 and I was rushed to ICU. It was determined that I had pneumonia and had almost gone into ARDS (acute respiratory distress syndrome). The doctors debated as to whether I should be put on a ventilator. Finally my pulmonary specialist, Dr. Paresh Timbadia, decided that due to my all around good health and sound lungs not to put me on the ventilator. After five days in ICU and two days in a regular room, I was released. I had to spend the next 17 weeks on oxygen which prevented me from attending the Penn State and Michigan games and five OSU basketball games. I also had to give away my tickets for the Michigan State and Purdue football road games. I was hooked up to an in-house oxygen unit and when I travelled I had to use a large portable tank that was only good for about an hour. Later in the basketball season I was able to attend the games using a small portable tank that was sufficient for four hours. I only needed to use it when I was walking. All of this misery and inconvenience could have been avoided if this male nurse named Tim had gotten me out of bed to walk during my time after surgery. He kept saying and I quote, "Boy I've got to get you up to walk or you're going to get pneumonia." He got me up once in four days and DUH, I got pneumonia. I wrote a letter to the Mount Carmel grievance committee and two months later I received a two page letter covering their rear ends. They claimed I was too weak to get up to walk. I told them I was not planning on getting an attorney and filing a law suit. I just wanted to make sure that Tim was reprimanded and wouldn't do this to another patient. So for the first time since 1978 I had to watch a home game with Michigan on television. It was a great game as Tressel won his third game in four years over our arch rival, something that his predecessor couldn't accomplish in 13 years. In that game Ted Ginn was outstanding and Troy Smith established himself as the Buckeye signal caller when he won his first of three straight over the Blue. Oh how I hated not being there in person for this great victory.

After the 2005 season in which the Bucks lost two close games to Texas and Penn State and finished the season 10 and 2, they were invited to the Fiesta Bowl for a BCS game with Notre Dame. I looked forward to this game as it would be the rubber match between these two storied programs. The Irish had prevailed in 1935 and 1936 with the Bucks being the victors more recently in 1995 and 1996. This game would be played on a neutral field in Tempe, Arizona, the site of the Bucks National Championship game in 2003. The Bucks were getting used to playing in the desert as they also defeated Kansas State in the 2004 BCS Fiesta Bowl. Leading up to the game there was all of this hype about Notre Dame's genius coach, Charlie Weis. The talk was if you give him five weeks to prepare for an opponent he will design a game plan that will make it hard to defeat his team. Well, guess what? The same could be said for Coach Jim Tressel. There was also much buzz about Notre Dame's golden boy quarterback Brady Quinn and how did such a talented player not go to Ohio State when he was in the Buckeye's back yard in Dublin, Ohio, a suburb of Columbus. All of the talking heads on ESPN, *Sports Illustrated*, and *Sporting News*, etc. indicated there was no way that Notre Dame with Weis as the coach and Quinn at quarterback would lose to the Buckeyes. There's an old saying, "You have to play the game!" Oh how those men of Scarlet and Gray did play as Troy outplayed Brady and Tressel out-coached Weis. I didn't attend the game. We got together with a bunch of friends and watched the game on their new HD television. It was a great evening as everyone was rooting for the Bucks and they didn't let us down. The Bucks now own the advantage 3 wins to 2 wins in the series.

You may recall that earlier in this book I spoke about one of my salesmen, who was a big Irish fan, and how he claimed that Woody was afraid to play Notre Dame; well it looks to me like the shoe is on the other foot. Notre Dame is now afraid to play the Buckeyes and that is why they don't want to join the Big Ten. In my opinion Big Ten teams like Michigan, Michigan State, and Purdue should refuse to play the Irish. Tell them if you want to schedule us, join the Big Ten.

There is always a lot of excitement leading up to the final game of the season with the Buckeyes arch rival Michigan, but the 2006 game provided even more excitement. The Bucks were ranked number one in the nation with the Wolverines coming in ranked second. Both teams were undefeated and loaded with talent. You could feel the tension in the air as the giant horseshoe was filled to capacity. The Buckeye fans were really rockin' and rollin' for this one. Seated in front of my nephew and I were two fans decked out in maize and blue. All through the game there was banter between us as the game swung back and forth between the two teams. In the end the Bucks won by three points, but actually should have won by ten. On Michigan's last touchdown drive the Wolverines benefited from a pass interference call which gave them new life. It happened right in front of us and it appeared to be a great defensive play, but the official called pass interference which gave Michigan a first down deep in the Bucks territory. Even the Michigan fans seated in front of us thought it was a bad call but as they said, "We'll take it." After the game Michigan running back Mike Hart was quoted as saying he didn't think the Buckeyes were that great and if they played them again Michigan would prevail easily. There was much talk about the two teams playing a rematch in the BCS Championship game in January. Michigan players and fans really wanted another crack at the Bucks and thought; due to the closeness of the game they deserved it. However, the Buckeye fans thought otherwise and so did the polls as the Florida Gators moved up to number two and were selected to play the Buckeyes for the title. In hindsight maybe we would have fared better against Michigan as the Gators upset the favored Buckeyes. Even though Florida spoiled the Bucks perfect season, the 2006 Michigan game will always be one of my favorites.

The next year the Bucks travelled to Ann Arbor to battle the Wolverines and mouthy Mike Hart and his teammates. Hart along with quarterback Chad Henne and offensive tackle Jake Long all decided to come back for their senior years instead of entering the NFL draft. Their reason, as big mouth Hart declared, was, "We are going to come back so we can go undefeated, win the national championship, and most of all beat those Buckeyes." That is the main reason for choosing the 2007 Michigan game as one of my all time favorites as the Bucks made Hart eat his words. Hart was ineffective running the ball and Henne had a bad day throwing the ball as OSU's Vernon Gholston provided pressure on him all afternoon. All-American Jake Long who had protected Henne's blind side as the left tackle, couldn't handle Gholston and gave up his first ever sack from that position. The Wolverines were held to a field goal as the Bucks prevailed 14 to 3 courtesy of running back "Beanie" Wells' two long touchdown runs. Hart was extremely quiet after that game as all he could think about was, in four years he never got to taste victory over the hated Buckeyes. We Buckeye fans knew how he felt as we suffered through the Cooper years. We tasted victory over the hated

Blue only two times. Many Buckeye players during those years never experienced the satisfaction of winning the Michigan game. During that time all we heard was how the Ohio State game wasn't Michigan's most important game; it was the Michigan State game or the Notre Dame game. I think they are singing a different tune since Coach Tressel arrived on the scene.

The 2008 game in Madison with the Wisconsin Badgers is my next favorite game for one reason. It was the coming of age of our highly recruited freshman, quarterback Terrelle Pryor. Just when it looked like the Bucks were headed for defeat Pryor led the team to the winning touchdown. My next favorite game is the 2009 game at Happy Valley with Penn State. After losing to a mediocre Purdue team in which Pryor was responsible for four of the Bucks five turnovers, it looked like the Bucks had no shot at winning the Big Ten title. However, with Iowa upsetting Penn State and Northwestern upsetting Iowa the Bucks had a chance for their fifth straight title. The schedule was difficult, on the road with Penn State, at home against Iowa and finish at Ann Arbor. Penn State, led by senior quarterback Daryll Clark and junior running back Evan Royster were explosive on offense. Ohio State's defensive end Cameron Heyward and linebacker Ross Homan led the defensive charge for the Buckeyes. Heyward spent more time in the Nittany Lions backfield than any of the Penn State players as he sacked Clark twice and pressured him all day. The Lions entered the game leading the Big Ten on offense, but the Bucks held the Lions to a season low 201 yards. The final score was 24 to 7. However the Lions first and only touchdown was tainted. Television replays showed that Clark's helmet broke the plane of the goal line but the ball did not as it was on his hip well short of the goal line. This was a special victory as the crowd was really harassing Pryor. They are still smarting over losing their native Pennsylvanian talent to the Bucks. It had to be especially satisfying for Pryor as it was his first trip back to his home state. He was also anxious to make up for the fumble the previous year which led to the touchdown that gave the Nittany Lions the win in Columbus. Tressel improved his record to 6 and 3 against Joe Pa. Even Cooper was 5 and 3 versus the coaching legend.

The November 14th encounter with the Iowa Hawkeyes was for all the marbles. A win over the Hawkeyes would clinch the Big Ten title and a trip to the Rose Bowl. It was a hard fought game which the Bucks won in overtime. The Bucks seemed to have the game wrapped up leading 24 to 10 but a kickoff return for a touchdown brought the Hawkeyes within seven points. The Buckeyes almost put the game out of reach when Thaddeus Gibson intercepted Iowa quarterback James Vandenberg's pass and ran it in for a touchdown. However, one of the Buckeyes was offside and the six points didn't count. OSU defensive tackle Doug Worthington came up with the big play in overtime when he sacked the Iowa quarterback which took the Hawkeyes out of field goal range. When Ohio State got in field goal range we Buckeye fans held our breath as the walk-on kicker was about to attempt the most important kick since he replaced the injured starting kicker Aaron Pettrey. When he booted a perfect kick the stadium crowd exploded. For the first time in 13 years the Buckeyes were Pasadena bound.

My last favorite game has to be the 2010 Rose Bowl win over the Oregon Ducks. This was my fourth trip to the Granddaddy of all the Bowls. I witnessed the Bucks lose three times to the Southern California Trojans in very close games, two of which cost the Bucks the national championship. My nephew Larry Mitchell and I had a great time during our time in California, but the victory was the icing on the cake. No one expected the Buckeyes to come out passing as that had not been the offensive strategy since the upset loss to Purdue. Tressel surprised everyone, especially the Ducks, with his wide open offense. Pryor was the MVP of the game and at long last displayed the talent that made him the most sought after recruit in the nation. We had excellent seats on about the 25 yard line with a great view of the game and the beautiful San Gabriel Mountains. Seated a few rows in front of us were Earle Bruce and his wife next to former OSU Athletic Director Jim Jones and his wife. I had this thought. Who made those seating arrangements? Jones was named AD by OSU President Ed Jennings when he agreed to fire Earle, something AD Rick Bay refused to do. I guess time heals. I feel bad for Earle. In two trips to the Rose Bowl he lost two heartbreakers to those damn Trojans of USC.

This was my nephew's and my first trip to a post season bowl since we were devastated by the 41 to 14 butt kicking that the Florida Gators gave our beloved Buckeyes in the 2007 BCS Championship game. Needless to say the trip home was more enjoyable than our last trip.

MY FAVORITE PLAYERS OF EACH DECADE.

The 1940s: Ollie Cline, Joe Whisler, Fred Morrison, Pandel Savic, and Bill Trautwein.

The 1950s: Vic Janowicz, Hop Cassady, Bob White, John Borton, Don Clark, and Dick LeBeau.

The 1960s: Bob Ferguson, Paul Warfield, Rex Kern, Ron Maciejowski, Jim Otis, Jack Tatum, Mike Sensibaugh, Jim Stillwagon and Bruce Jankowski.

The 1970s: Archie Griffin, Corny Greene, Pete Johnson, Brian Baschnagel, Tim Fox, Tom Skladany, Art Schlichter, Gary Williams and Doug Donley.

The 1980s: Vaughn Broadnax, Cris Carter, Chris Spielman, Keith Byars, John Frank and Marcus Marek

The 1990s: Kirk Herbstreit, Joey Galloway, Korey Stringer, Orlando Pace, Eddie George, Terry Glenn, Shawn Springs, Antoine Winfield and Joe Germaine.

The 2000s: Troy Smith, Nate Clements, Chris Gamble, Ted Ginn, Jr., Matt Wilhelm, Anthony Gonzalez, Nick Mangold, Michael Jenkins, Mike Doss, A.J. Hawk, Mike Nugent, Santonio Holmes, Malcolm Jenkins, and Brian Rolle.

MY ALL-TIME BUCKEYES BY POSITION AND TOP COACHES

Quarterbacks:

1. Troy Smith	4. Joe Germaine
2. Rex Kern	5. Corny Greene
3. Art Schlichter	

Running Backs:

1. Vic Janowicz	4. Eddie George
2. Hop Cassady	5. Keith Byars
3. Archie Griffin	

Fullbacks:

1. Pete Johnson
2. Bob Ferguson
3. Bob White
4. Jim Otis
5. John Brockington

Tight Ends:

1. Jan White
2. John Frank
3. Rickey Dudley
4. Ben Hartsock
5. Jim Houston

Receiver:

1. Cris Carter
2. Gary Williams
3. David Boston
4. Ted Ginn, Jr.
5. Michael Jenkins
6. Chris Gamble
7. Santonio Holmes
8. Anthony Gonzalez
9. Doug Donley
10. Joey Galloway

Offensive Lineman:

1. Jim Parker
2. Orlando Pace
3. Korey Stringer
4. Dave Foley
5. Rufus Mayes
6. Francis Machinsky
7. Tom Deleone
8. Jim Lachey
9. Kirk Lowdermilk
10. Nick Mangold

Defense Lineman:

1. Jim Parker
2. Dan Wilkinson
3. Mike Vrabel
4. Jim Stillwagon (Middle Guard)
5. Vernon Gholston

Linebacker:

1. Chris Spielman
2. Randy Gradishar
3. Tom Cousineau
4. A.J. Hawk
5. Jim Laurinaitis

Cornerback:

1. Jack Tatum
2. Shawn Springs
3. Chris Gamble

4. Neal Colzie
5. Antoine Winfield

Safety:

1. Tim Fox
2. Mike Sensibaugh
3. Mike Doss

4. Damon Moore
5. Will Allen

Punter:

1. Tom Skladany
2. Andy Groom

3. B.J. Sander
4. Vic Janowicz

Kicker:

1. Mike Nugent
2. Vlade Janakievski

3. Tom Klaban
4. Vic Janowicz

Coach:

I would have to rate Woody Hayes as the best OSU head coach with Jim Tressel a close second. Although I never saw him coach I would have to rank Francis Schmidt as my choice for number three, based on two factors. First he was the first coach to defeat Michigan four straight times and all four were shutouts. The second reason was he created the gold pants award for defeating that team up north. Next I would select Earle Bruce who in just nine years had a winning record against Michigan and had a winning bowl record. When he was fired he had .755 record second only to Woody's .761 and he had the difficult task of succeeding a legend. My fifth coach is John Cooper, who in spite of his inability to defeat Michigan and win bowl games, did post a .715 record in his thirteen years as the head coach. He was without a doubt an outstanding recruiter and did provide this long time Buckeye fan with some memorable victories. The 1997 Rose Bowl win over Arizona State, the winning record against Joe Pa's Nittany Lions and the two wins over Lou Holtz's "Fighting' Irish" are some that I will always treasure.

Chapter 27

My Final Thoughts About This Book And Other Books

As I come to the end of my thoughts, memories and opinions as a die-hard Buckeye fan, I hope that what I have written is more accurate than some of the books I have read about the Buckeyes. The following books are ones in which I found numerous errors: "Woody's Boys," "What It Means to Be a Buckeye," "I Remember Woody," "Great Moments in Ohio State Football History," "A Fire to Win, The Life and Times of Woody Hayes," "Earle a Coach's Life," and "Game of My Life." I wrote to the publishers informing them of the mistakes, and I'm not talking about typos, but factual errors. I only received a response from two of them, Orange Frazer Press in Wilmington, Ohio, and Laura Lanese, the co-author of "Game of My Life." Orange Frazer thanked me for the errors I found in their book, "Woody's Boys." They stated in their letter, "Obviously, we hired the wrong proofreader." They went on to say that they didn't realize how faulty the memories of the players were. "We found errors by the dozens, and still missed the ones you found." Some of the errors in that book were as follows: former player Billy Joe Armstrong was quoted as saying "There was a great group of guys there then. You had Lou Holtz, Earle Bruce and George Chaump." Armstrong played in 1960-61-62. Lou Holtz was defensive backfield coach at Ohio State for only one season, 1968. Earle Bruce was an assistant coach under Woody for six seasons, 1966 thru 1972. As you can see neither coach was there when Billy Joe was there. Another error was concerning Wes Fesler resigning as head coach. In the book it states that he resigned after the Rose Bowl in 1950. In the next paragraph it states that Fesler resigned at the Big Ten meetings in 1949. Ohio State won the Rose Bowl on January 1, 1950, and Fesler resigned near the end of 1950. He was nearly run out of town by the Buckeye fans and Russ Needham, the Sports Editor of the *Columbus Dispatch*, for punting on third down in the 1950 "Snow Bowl" game with Michigan. In that same paragraph it indicates that Paul Bixler, the coach that Fesler succeeded at OSU, returned to Cornell as head coach. Bixler went to Colgate as head coach and later joined Paul Brown with the Cleveland Browns. In the chapter on Paul Hornung of the *Columbus Dispatch*, there were several minor errors that only a devoted fan like me would notice. However, when talking about head coach Francis Schmidt he didn't mention that in his first four seasons he not only defeated the hated Wolverines of Michigan, but he shut them out all four years. Then he lost to them the next three years and he was history. No OSU head football coach has ever retained his job after losing three straight to Michigan, including Woody, until John Cooper did. One final correction is in the time line in the back of the book under the 1970s. It states under the 1974 season that OSU's loss to USC in the 1975 Rose Bowl was their only defeat and it cost them the national title. This is inaccurate. The Buckeyes lost to Michigan State 16 to 13 in the regular season in a very controversial ending, when the officials disallowed a last second touchdown by "Champ" Henson. Henson talks about this in the chapter on Henson in the book.

In the book entitled "EARLE A Coach's Life" I found the following errors: In describing the 1971 game in Ann Arbor with Michigan it states that "Michigan defensive back Thom Darden came through the line and fouled our receiver, Dick Wakefield." What actually happened was our receiver went over the middle behind the Michigan defensive line and Darden climbed over Wakefield's back to intercept the ball and end the Buckeye's last chance scoring threat as they trailed by three in the game. The book goes on to say it was offensive pass interference, and we lost the game 10 to 7. It wasn't offensive pass interference; it was obviously defensive pass interference instead of an interception as the official ruled. That is why Woody went ballistic and tore up the sideline markers. The book tells of Earle's great victory over the hated Blue in the Big House in his first year in 1979. The book states, "That victory broke the jinx of not scoring in three years." It is true that in Woody's last three years the Bucks had not scored a touchdown against "That Team up North," but they did score on them: six points in 1977 by way of two field goals and three points in Woody's last year in 1978. On page 126 the book states that Mike Tomczak threw a touchdown pass to Thad Jemison on the last play of the game. I attended that Fiesta Bowl game and it was one of the greatest thrills of my years of being a rabid Buckeye fan. However, that pass was not the last play of the game. There was still time left in the game and the Buckeyes had to kick off to Pittsburgh. They were moving the ball when their quarterback got injured and left the game. The Bucks defense stopped them and Ohio State won 28 to 23.

The last error in the book is where it states that Art Schlichter grew up in Washington Court House. He grew up in Bloomingburg, Ohio, which is near Washington Court House. He broke all school records as a quarterback at Miami Trace High School which is located in Washington Court House. Incidentally this book was also published by Orange Frazer Press, however this time they did not respond to my letter about this book.

Triumph Books in Chicago was the publisher of "What It Means to Be a Buckeye," "I Remember Woody," and "Great Moments in Ohio State Football History." I wrote to them and informed them of errors in their books. I received no response! Here are the errors in "What It Means to Be a Buckeye." On page 16 they misspelled the name of the downtown Columbus main hotel. It was the Deshler-Wallick not the Deshler. On that same page they refer to the University Theater as being off Neil Ave. It was on High Street. Today it is a McDonald's fast food restaurant. On page 37 they refer to Howard "Hopalong" Cassady's high school coach as Howell. His name was Frank Howe. In the 1974 loss to Michigan State it was "Champ" Henson who went into the end zone as time expired, not Archie Griffin. On page 183 Ken Fritz makes the statement that Clemson's Charlie Bauman got in Woody's face which caused Woody's reaction. The TV replay of the incident that led to Woody's firing clearly shows that this never happened. Bauman had his back to Woody and Woody turned him around and slugged him. On page 194 quarterback "Corny" Greene is quoted as saying the 1974 loss to Michigan State was the only regular loss in his four years as a Buckeye. This isn't true, as the Spartans also upset the Bucks in 1972 at East Lansing 19 to 12 to ruin the Scarlet and Gray's undefeated regular season. Greene was not the quarterback in 1972; it was Greg Hare. Maybe "Corny" was thinking it was his only regular season loss as a starting quarterback. On page 223 Cal Murray is recalling the 1979 Michigan game in Ann Arbor and he states it was the first time we scored a touchdown in their stadium in four years. This is inaccurate as it was the first time the Bucks had scored a touchdown against Michigan in four years period. The 1976 and 1978 games were played in Columbus and the Bucks were shut out 22 to 0 in '76 and 14 to 3 in '78. In 1977 the Bucks lost 14 to 6 (two field goals). Prior to that the Bucks in Ann Arbor scored three touchdowns in a 21 to 14 victory in 1975 and scored one touchdown in a 10 to 10 tie in 1973.

The errors in the book "I Remember Woody" began on page 12 where they quoted Archie Griffin as saying, "I started the next game against North Carolina. If I had known I was going to start and had been with the team at the hotel the night before the game, I might've been a nervous wreck!" Archie did not start the North Carolina game. Morris Bradshaw was the starting tailback and after the Buckeyes had only gained 13 yards on their first two possessions, Woody, at the urging of assistant coach Rudy Hubbard, decided to give the freshman Griffin a shot. I was at the game and I witnessed Archie break Ollie Cline's school record with 239 yards. I know Archie to be a man of integrity, and I can't believe he told the authors that he started the game. It appears that the authors, Steve Greenberg and Dale Raterman got it wrong. On page 60, it states John Hicks as saying that when he was a starter the Bucks finished 19-2-1. Hicks was a starter in 1970, 1972, and 1973. He sat out 1971 due to an injury. In the '70, '72, and '73 seasons the Buckeyes finished 28-3-1. On page 194, on the section about Dan Devine, it states that Ohio State tied Michigan for the Big Ten title in 1973, but Michigan went to the Rose Bowl. Ohio State and Michigan played to a 10 to 10 tie that year, and also tied for the title. The Big Ten Athletic Directors voted, much to the chagrin of Bo Schembechler, to send Ohio State to the Rose Bowl. Ohio State represented the Big Ten well and made the AD's decision look good with a convincing win over the USC Trojans 42 to 21.

In reading "Greatest Moments in Ohio State Football History" I found the following errors. On page 44 it was stated that the Buckeyes lost to California in the 1921 Rose Bowl, 18 to 0. The actual score was 28 to 0. On pages 44-45 it states that the 1950 Rose Bowl was Head Coach Wes Fesler's last collegiate game that he coached. There are two errors here. First, Fesler didn't resign until after the infamous Snow Bowl, which was played in Columbus in November 1950. This was over 11 months and 9 games after the 1950 Rose Bowl game. In the book it states that after resigning he went into business in Minnesota. However, he later became head coach of the Minnesota Gophers. He not only coached nine games at Ohio State, but additional games at Minnesota, therefore the claim that the 1950 Rose Bowl was the last college game he coached is totally false. On page 47 it states that Vic Janowicz kicked a field goal in the 1950 Snow Bowl game with the wind. This is also wrong. Janowicz's kick was into the teeth of a stiff winter wind in the midst of heavy snow. That is why his kick was considered so great. On page 68 the caption under the picture indicates No. 18 is quarterback Frank Kremblas scoring a touchdown. Kremblas was Caucasian. The number 18 in the picture is half back Don Clark who was African-American. On page 79 it indicates that Ohio State defeated Southern California 17 to 14 in the 1950 Rose Bowl, when it was California that they defeated. On page 117 the caption under the picture should read "The Buckeyes would lose three out of four trips to Pasadena during Griffin's era, not two of three as stated in the book." The Bucks won in 1974 and lost in 1973, 1975, and 1976 in the Jan. 1st Rose Bowls when Archie Griffin played for the Bucks. On page 142 it states OSU was clinging to a 7 to 6 lead in the fourth quarter before it started its punishing assault. In the box score at the top of the page it clearly shows that the score was 21 to 6 at the end of the third quarter and the fourth quarter was scoreless in the 1984 game with Michigan at Ohio Stadium. On page 204 it indicates that OSU's eight defeats by Michigan under head coach John Cooper cost them four national championship runs. It was only three, 1993, 1995, and 1996. The fourth one was blown by a loss to Michigan State, not Michigan in 1998.

In all, I wrote three letters to Triumph Books about these errors and I never heard a peep from them. It really bothers me that many people read these books believing everything written in them, when there were so many inaccuracies within those pages.

This brings me to the book "A Fire to Win, The Life and Times of Woody Hayes" published by St. Martin's Press in New York, N.Y. In this book I found these errors. On page 82 it states that "Wes Fesler remains the only Ohio State coach who stopped coaching the Buckeyes without being fired." This is just not true. Paul Brown left after the 1943 season without being fired. Carroll Widdoes resigned after the 1945 season and his successor, Paul Bixler departed after one season in 1946 to become head coach at Colgate where there was less pressure. John Lombardo, the author, himself confirms his error on page 82 when on the next page (83) he states that Francis Schmidt left under pressure and Paul Brown was hired. Also he states on that same page (83) that when Paul Brown became head coach at Cleveland in the All America Conference it paved the way for Fesler to become head coach in 1947. Paul Brown left in 1943, followed by Carroll Widdoes, who coached for two seasons, 1944 and 1945 who was then succeeded by Bixler in 1946. In several places in the book, the author refers to Miami University of Ohio as the Indians. They were never called by that name. They were the Redskins until recently when the name was changed to the Red Hawks because of objections by Native Americans to the term Redskins. On page 97 the author states that Woody encountered a disheveled Janowicz at a hotel in Chicago before a game with Northwestern in Evanston, Illinois. After the game he put Janowicz on a plane to Columbus and arranged for his rehabilitation from the brain damage he suffered in an auto accident in Los Angeles. He states the year was 1954. This is impossible as Janowicz's accident happened in 1956 as he so states in the previous paragraph. On page 101 Mr. Lombardo states that Woody couldn't keep "Hop" Cassady off the field, when the Buckeyes opened the 1953 season." It was the 1952 season when Cassady was a freshman and he scored three touchdowns against Indiana. On page 117 Lombardo states "when it's first and goal on your own six inch line," ... It can't be first and goal on your own six inch line. It would either be first and goal on the opponent's six inch line or first and ten on your own six inch line.

On page 181 in the second paragraph he states, "though it was just the second game of the season ... The Purdue game he is referring to was the third game of the 1968 season. The first game was against SMU and the second game opponent was the Oregon Ducks. On page 185 the mayor of Columbus was Maynard Sensenbrenner not James Sensenbrenner. James Rhodes was a former mayor of Columbus and was the governor of Ohio at the time. On page 108 it was not Texas that the Buckeyes defeated in their home opener in 1970, 56 to 13. It was Texas A&M. The Buckeyes played Texas for the first time in 2005. On page 236 in the second paragraph the game was in the Gator Bowl not the Citrus Bowl. He got it right in one sentence and then wrong in the next sentence. On page 243 it indicates that Woody took an office in St. John Arena just north of Woody Hayes Dr. At that time it was not named Woody Hayes Dr. but Woodruff Dr. They changed the name in his honor after he died in 1987. On page 251 it states that Woody gave the commencement address at the school's 259th commencement ceremonies on March 21, 1987. That would not have been possible as Woody passed away on March 12, 1987. (The commencement address was actually March 21, 1986.)

Laura Lanese, wife of Mike Lanese, an outstanding flanker for the Buckeyes in 1984 and 1985, is the co-author of the book, "Game of My Life." She collaborated with Steve Greenberg who also wrote "I Remember Woody." Mike, a Rhodes Scholar, will always be remembered in Buckeye lore for his sensational catch in the 1984 Michigan game which led to a Buckeye victory over the "hated Blue." Instead of writing to the publisher, Sports Publishing LLC, I decided to write to the two authors. I did not hear from Greenberg, which was no surprise as he had not responded to my previous letter about the errors in the book "I Remember Woody." I did receive an email from Mrs. Lanese and she was very appreciative of my informing her of the errors. She indicated that she was most embarrassed about the error about A.J. Hawk. She went on to say that she only wished that I had written sooner before the second printing of the book. During the second printing they were able to correct some other factual errors, not including mine, as well as some typographical ones. She indicated that she would add my corrections to the next printing.

These are the errors I found in "Game of My Life." On the first page about A.J. Hawk it states that among other awards in 2005 he won the Butkus Award. He did not, although he should have. Instead it went to Paul Poluskany of Penn State. On page 140 about Demetrius Stanley it states, "Joey Galloway threw a post route across the middle to me, and I ran it in for a 72 yd. touchdown." Joey Galloway was a slot-end and he last played for the Bucks in 1994. This game was the 1997 Rose Bowl. The quarterbacks for Ohio State were Stanley Jackson and Joe Germaine. Germaine led the winning drive and threw the winning touchdown to David Boston, who was the slot-end at the time. As I recall the pass to Demetrius was thrown by Stanley Jackson. On page 152 it states that Floyd Stahl was an assistant coach in the infamous Snow Bowl game with Michigan. Stahl, the former head basketball coach, was an assistant athletic director at that time. At the top of page 172 it refers to the Oklahoma fans as rabid OSU fans. Oklahoma fans are OU fans. OSU is Oklahoma State fans. On page 177 Vic Koegel recalls the Rose Bowl game of 1974 and states that Southern Cal had beaten us the year before and had killed us the year before that. This is incorrect. It was the year before (1973) that Southern Cal whipped the Bucks 42 to 17. The year before that the Bucks were not in the Rose Bowl (1972). It was the year before that, 1971, that the Bucks were upset 27 to 17 by Stanford. On page 179 it states the score was tied at half-time 14 to 14. Then it states that the Trojans opened the third quarter with an 83 yard touchdown drive to give USC a 21 to 17 lead. When did Ohio State get the 3 points? On page 198 it talks about Vaughn Broadnax's block in the Michigan game at Ann Arbor in 1981. In the last paragraph it states, "With time winding down, Broadnax flattened one Michigan defender, allowing Ohio State quarterback Art Schlichter to get loose for the winning touchdown." The reason everyone remembers the block thrown by Broadnax was because he didn't flatten one Michigan defender, but three defenders with one block. I was there and I remember it well, as do all Buckeye fans. To say he blocked one defender does not explain why the block is legendary in the annals of OSU football history. On page 203 it wasn't Elmer Lippert that Archie Griffin replaced in the North Carolina game, it was Morris Bradshaw. Bradshaw had been ineffective in the game. After Archie's great record breaking performance, Bradshaw switched to wide receiver and went on to have a great career in the NFL. On page 222 it states in 1993 it was John Cooper's first bowl game as OSU coach. This is incorrect; it was Cooper's first bowl victory as OSU head coach. Prior to that Holiday Bowl win over BYU he lost to Auburn and Syracuse in the "Hall of Fame Bowl" and to Air Force in the "Liberty Bowl."

The reason that I wrote to the publishers and authors of these books was to prevent people who engage in OSU football trivia from basing their answers on incorrect facts contained in these books. In 2009 I went to the Purdue game in West Lafayette, Indiana. The heavy underdog Boilermakers upset the Buckeyes due mainly to five turnovers. My nephew and I travelled by bus with Travel Pals of Dublin, Ohio. The only bright spot of the trip was when I won the trivia contest on the bus trip over to Ross-Ade Stadium. The prize was a book on OSU trivia. When I returned home I read this book and found it too contained many errors. I wrote to the author Mike McGuire, who self-published this book, and listed the errors that I discovered in his book. His reply was "thanks for your e-mail, and I will check my records." I never heard back from him. I won't list all of the errors at this time, but there were a couple that I thought were noteworthy. Two times in his book he refers to Woody resigning as head coach of the Bucks. He did not resign, he was fired. AD Hugh Hindman asked him to resign after the incident at the 1978 Gator Bowl, but he refused and stated, "You will have to fire me!" And Hindman did! He indicated that John Cooper's bowl record was 4 and 7, when it was 3 and 8. His only victories were in the 1993 Holiday Bowl, the 1997 Rose Bowl and the 1999 Sugar Bowl. One of his trivia questions was, "In what four Rose Bowls was Ohio State undefeated?" His answer was 1950, 17 to 14 over California; 1955, 20 to 7 USC, 1958, 10 to 7 Oregon, 1969, 27 to 16 USC. The Buckeyes were not undefeated in 1950 (1949 season 7-1-2) and 1958 (1957 season 9-1 as they lost the home opener to TCU 17 to 14.) The Buckeyes were undefeated in the 1954 and 1968 seasons and won both Rose Bowls. In 1973 they had an undefeated season with a 10 to 10 tie with Michigan and they won the Rose Bowl. In 1979 and 1975 they had an undefeated regular season but lost both Rose Bowls. In the 2007 Ohio State vs. Michigan game he had the final score 20 to 3, when it was actually 14 to 3 as Beanie Wells scored both touchdowns on long runs from scrimmage.

As you read this book and you discover any factual errors that I have made, I would appreciate it if you would call them to my attention via the publisher. I will do my best to respond personally.

Epilogue

When I originally wrote the epilogue for this book it was prior to the start of the 2011 football season. Now that the 2011 season is history I decided to devote my epilogue to this forgettable season. It ended with a 6 and 6 record and an opportunity to go 7 and 6 with a win in the Gator Bowl over a 6 and 6 Florida team.

In looking back on this season instead of posting a 6 and 6 record the Bucks could have easily finished with a respectable 9 and 3 record or even 10 and 2. When I think of those games there are at least 3 or 4 losses that could have been wins. There were games that I could have added to my "What if?" chapter. The first one that comes to mind is the Nebraska game. The Buckeye offense was having its way with the Husker defense until quarterback Braxton Miller had to leave the game with a leg injury. His replacement Joe Bauserman, was totally ineffective, as was the play calling from that point on as they kept having Bauserman throw deep. Throwing deep is not Bauserman's strength. If only Miller hadn't been injured I believe the Bucks would have come out on top.

The next winnable game was the Purdue game. If the extra point had not been blocked it would have been a great come-from-behind win. There were two key plays that could have put the Penn State game in the win column. Corey Brown's drop of an excellent pass on the Penn State 15 yard line killed a good drive. Later in the fourth quarter the Bucks faced a fourth and five in Penn State territory when right tackle Shuggarts was called for an illegal procedure, a penalty that he committed at least once in every game. There are a lot more options when facing fourth and five instead of fourth and ten. In the ensuing play Miller scrambled for nine yards, falling a yard short of a first down. The Nittany Lions took over and ran out the clock. If Brown doesn't drop that pass ... if only? If Shuggarts doesn't draw that penalty ... if only?

Finally in the Michigan game with one minute and 29 seconds remaining in the game and Michigan leading 40 to 34, Miller overthrows a wide open Devier Posey. If Miller doesn't overthrow Posey ... if only? Instead of a 10 and 2 season and a possible BCS bowl bid the Bucks posted a 6 and 6 record and an invitation to the Gator Bowl.

The next month the NCAA handed down their decision for Ohio State's infractions during the 2010 season. The shocker was the bowl ban for the 2012 season. Athletic Director Gene Smith was confident that the Bucks wouldn't get a bowl ban. With his past experience with the NCAA everyone believed him. In retrospect Ohio State should have turned down the Gator Bowl invitation and just maybe the NCAA would not have banned the Buckeyes from a bowl in 2012.

I found it hard to believe that Dan Herron and Posey would get further suspensions due to their accepting money for work they didn't perform. How could they do this after the tattoo incident? I would like to have seen Luke Fickell kick both of them off the team.

Speaking of Fickell, I thought he did a good job as interim head coach considering all that he inherited. He had to live with a coaching staff that was not of his choosing. With an inept offensive coordinator, a quarterback coach who had previously served as a video coordinator, and finally the ex-coach's brother as the running back coach and special team coach; the deck was stacked against Fickell.

I did question some of Fickell's decisions. First not playing Miller in the Toledo game made no sense at all, as the young freshman needed experience before heading down to play the Miami Hurricanes. His faith in Bauserman was unbelievable. I thought he should have benched him and given Kenny Guiton reps in practice and installed him as Miller's backup.

It wasn't all bad news in 2011 as Urban Meyer was named head coach for 2012. He signed a four-year contract estimated to be four million dollars per year. I'm sure Meyer will return the Bucks to one of the elite programs, despite the bowl ban they will face next year. Our bowl will be the Michigan game as the Bucks start a new winning streak against the hated Blue.

The Gator Bowl loss to Florida was painful as the Bucks continue to lose to the SEC teams. (Last year's win over Arkansas has been vacated.) The Bucks played the Gators pretty much even with the exception of the two special team touchdowns. Miller overthrowing a wide open Posey in the end zone caused the Bucks to settle for a field goal. Instead of being tied at 14 to 14 the Bucks trailed 14 to 10 at the half. The killer was the blocked punt for a touchdown in the third quarter and the defense failing to make a stop when Florida ran six minutes off the clock in the fourth quarter. I don't think I have ever seen, in all of my years of following the Bucks, such inept play by special teams as I witnessed in the Bucks seventh loss of a very forgettable season.

Better days await the Ohio State Buckeyes as they prepare for another era called the Urban Era.

Finally, I hope you have enjoyed reading this book as much I have in writing it.

1. Me & Earle
   Bruce

2. Me & Mike
   Tomzcak, 1984

3. Keith Byars,
   1984

4. Me & Vaughn
   Broadnax,
   1982

5. Coach Hayes at a Senior Tackle

1. *Me*

2. *Me & Howard "Hopalong" Cassady, 2005*

3. *Coach Tressel*

4. *Rose Parade*

1. Me at age 14

2. Ohio Stadium of old

3. Sunday Newsman, WHOK, Lancaster, OH

4. All-night DJ, WHOK

5. Marty & Me, prom

6. Me & Marty, 1970s

7. View of Schottenstein Center from the 'Shoe'

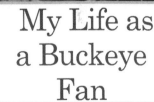

My Life as a Buckeye Fan

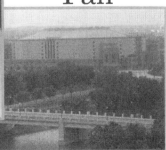

Made in the USA
Charleston, SC
11 November 2012